T0194947

Evidence of God

Shirley Hall

authorHOUSE®

AuthorHouse™
1663 Liberty Drive
Bloomington, IN 47403
www.authorhouse.com
Phone: 1 (800) 839-8640

Scripture taken from The Holy Bible, King James Version. Public Domain

Scripture quotations marked NKJV are taken from the New King James Version. Copyright © 1982 by Thomas Nelson, Inc. Used by permission. All rights reserved.

Published by AuthorHouse 06/26/2019

ISBN: 978-1-7283-1691-8 (sc)
ISBN: 978-1-7283-1690-1 (e)

Print information available on the last page.

ACKNOWLEDGEMENT

Thanks to:
Janet Greider for all her wisdom and editing,
Sara Roberts for her encouragement,
Elaine Lee for her help,
Laura Beldon for her tweaking ability,
And to my mother who was a great inspiration.

CONTENTS

FOREWORD

Can you imagine sitting in front of the King of Kings, the one living God, being consumed with His peace and love, being consumed with His presence? This is something I could never even begin to wrap my mind around. The day when that comes will be such a feeling I have always longed for. What if the Holy Spirit wanted us to experience that now? What if we were missing out on experiencing the presence of God right here on earth?

Watching my mother my whole life tap into the presence of God has been an amazing experience. She has been walking with the Lord for thirty-four years and she has always been on fire for God. She has had many encounters with God, and as her daughter, I was able to be one of the first people she told about her experiences. Growing up, I can remember waking up early and my mom was always upstairs reading the Bible or praying in her prayer language. As I would come up the stairs, she would finish her time with God, and she would often have a dream or something very cool that God had told her or shown her that day. I never quite understood what everything meant or why God would show my mother such cool things. However, as an adult and after reading this book, I can remember back when these things **actually took place**. What I know now is that God was teaching my mother how to hear his voice and how to have a relationship with Him.

I wasn't always so excited about the Lord. Trust me! For a long time, I wanted nothing to do with Him. Even growing up in a wonderful Spirit-filled home, I strayed far away. My mother played a huge role in me giving my life back to Christ. If she hadn't prayed for me for so many years, I'm not sure I would be writing this today. I could never thank her enough for not losing faith in me. My mother is my best friend and now we get to be excited about Jesus together. She has shown me an example of what truly being in love with the Lord looks like. She has spent her lifetime enjoying the richness of His presence right here on earth!

I strongly hope that after reading this book you can begin to seek God like never before. I pray that your heart will begin to be open to all the things that God has intended for you to experience. I encourage you to start asking the Lord to give you dreams, visions, understanding, wisdom, and most importantly how to have a deep and intimate relationship with Him. I have learned how to do these things by watching my mom and by taking her advice. My mother's life has always been a living testament to me, and I know I strive to be just like her.

Sara Roberts
(Daughter)

CHAPTER 1

Evidence That God Commissions To Write

With a prayer book and several unpublished children's books collecting dust in a corner, writing another book was not a commission I was expecting. I hadn't gotten these other books off my plate when the Lord called me to another project. Experience has shown me that God can and often interrupts our best laid plans. He catches me off guard every time he does something big in my life, surprising me in the most wonderful of ways. I dearly love those sudden interruptions.

It all started during a long drive to a conference with a friend. As I checked the mail before leaving, I noticed a biography of one of my favorite speakers, Tom Horn, had arrived. He was one of the scheduled speakers that weekend, so I tucked the book in the van.

Laura, my book worm companion, noticed the book as I placed it in the van. We share a love of books, but where she devours books from cover to cover, I found that I had fallen into a habit of picking and choosing parts of several books at a time, but never seeming to finish any of them. So, this was a perfect set up for us both.

It was an eight-hour drive, so Laura suggested reading his book out loud to pass the time. She was just as interested in learning more about the man we were going to hear speak. As she was reading the book, a very strange occurrence started happening. My life experiences kept flashing before me; one encounter after another replaying in my mind. Massive amounts of memories were flooding me, some of which were long ago and some long since forgotten. The Holy Spirit was stirring me by reminding me of all that God had done in my life.

By the time we were half-way home, I found myself astonished at all the times God had moved in my life. I did not want to sound presumptuous, but I turned to Laura in excitement and shared my thoughts that I could write a story of my life. I had refrained from speaking this to her the entire trip until now. No sooner than the words were out of my mouth, my eyes were drawn past my friend to a gigantic billboard on the side of the road with big black letters that said, "Continue Your Story!" I was astonished!

I thought, "Okay Lord, I get it!" I was finally taking the hint. God was sending me a sign, literally. He perfectly timed my words to Laura with an immediate giant-sized confirmation! The Lord wanted me to write a book of the complete story of my life and all that He had done. It was just another fascinating way God had shown Himself during my Christian life.

After five months, jotting notes of all the times the Lord did something noteworthy, I had four pages of notes. That was a great start, but way short of the book God gave me vision for. I found myself stuck asking God questions like – how do I write this? How do I organize this? What should the focus be? How do you put thirty-four years of experiences in a book?

It was another month later, while lying in bed early one morning, the Lord spoke the title of the book, "Evidence of God." I could hardly contain my excitement; this was such a breakthrough for me. Each of these events in my life were in fact, evidences of God. The title was perfect and once again, God demonstrated to me the evidence of Him in my life. The next step to moving forward in this project was how would I organize it. Again, a lifetime of evidence was going to be difficult to organize.

Two days later, once again while lying in bed, the Lord answered my next question. Each chapter was to be an evidence of who he has proven to be by my personal experiences. It is almost unimaginable at how impressed I was with yet another perfect plan that God had given me. I still wonder at how He continues to be evident in my daily life. He gave me exactly what I needed to get started. It was going to be easier than I thought! I just needed to write the stories and put them in the right chapter. An almost impossible task made virtually effortless is yet another evidence of God!

Now to Him who is able to do exceedingly abundantly above all that
we ask or think, according to the power that works in us (Eph. 3:20)

Although God had confirmed the commission and given me clear
direction, He gave me yet another confirmation through church. For
weeks, our pastor emphasized the importance of our individual stories. We
each have a testimony of God's faithfulness. When God takes the time to
confirm a direction, He gives us the way to move forward in confidence.
What is your story what could He be commissioning you to do?

My experience has proven to me that God never issues an assignment
without giving direction on how to accomplish it. As we seek him, He
is easily found. Assuredly, it might take some time, but God is always
faithful to supply what we need. His timing is perfect and flows according
to His purpose. Just think, God chose us to make us His dwelling place.
Therefore, as we listen and have patience, God will order our direction and
provide the means to walk it out.

The Spirit of truth, whom the world cannot receive, because
it neither sees Him nor knows Him; but you know Him, for
He dwells with you and will be in you. John 14:17

CHAPTER 2

Overview -
What a Wonderful Life

Did you ever believe something and then find out it was wrong? As a young woman I started believing a lie regarding the 'Jesus story'. I began to consider that it was just a fable. There were fairy tales, make-believe movies and just about any fantasy story out there that you can imagine. This caused me to consider the possibility that, just maybe, Jesus was not real and was part of man's creation. I was starting to come to that point of unbelief and that is just what the enemy wanted!

But, thankfully, God was right there to lead me back to truth!

God knows what we are thinking, and He knows what the enemy is lying to us about. Amazingly, He is right there to counter the enemies lies. What is so incredible is that God knows where we are spiritually and detects when we have had enough of life without Him. I believe it is at that point that the Holy Spirit begins to draw us to the Father. At a young age, I accepted the Lord and then I went in my own direction for quite some time. It was like I was living life going down a long winding road and then I ended up on a dead-end street. I was trying to fill a void in my life with drugs, alcohol and men. All those things served as a temporary filling, but only God could fill the emptiness I was experiencing. Eventually, God began to fill me with a desire for Him redirecting me for His greater purpose. He let me wander in that world without Him just long enough to realize it did not have much to offer in way of peace, joy or fulfillment. All that changed when Jesus made Himself known to me.

My life was never the same after the Lord rescued me from myself. He showed me the difference between living for myself and living for Him. It truly was like night and day. He turned on the lights and I began to see life differently. The person that wrote "Amazing Grace" knew what they were talking about as they wrote the words proclaiming…I was blind and now I see. The confusion went away, and I began to enjoy life once again. I had no idea how much fun I would have in the coming years learning how to walk in His ways and getting to know Him.

From that final turning point it has been such a wonderful life!

From the beginning of my Christian walk I saw many evidences of God. I saw evidence where God revealed His character. They were like an endless trail of exciting treasures just waiting to be dug up and discovered. I am a firm believer that the Lord is looking for those who truly seek after Him. As we run after Him, He begins to bring us into His world and shows us what He is all about.

For the eyes of the LORD run to and fro throughout the whole earth, to show Himself strong on behalf of those whose heart is loyal to Him. (2Chron16:9)

The more I experienced with the Lord, the more I wanted. It was an exciting journey from the beginning and after 34 years is still very exciting. The Lord gave me the title for this book, and it is a perfect title. As I began to have doubts of His existence, I presume He decided to show me evidence that He did exist. The following chapters will depict various testimonies that proved to me that God is loving, caring and is present in our daily lives. I have always had great anticipation concerning God because He has filled my life with surprises. It says that He stands at the door and knocks. He is waiting for us to open the door that directly leads to Him and to let Him in. I find that the more I open myself to Him the more He reveals Himself and His kingdom. God has shown me His faithfulness at every step of the way which has aided my ability to trust Him. I have learned to trust Him and know He is always working in my behalf moving me toward His kingdom purposes.

Living this Christian life has been above and beyond what I **ever** could have dreamed of or could have comprehended. I wish we could completely grasp the concept of who He is and what is available as believers, immediately, but it sometimes seems to take a lifetime. It probably will take an eternity to know all of God's attributes! I accredit my strength as a Christian all to Him! From the beginning of my personal relationship with Jesus He made Himself known. I got to know Him through His word, dreams and visions, people, signs, nature, and by hearing His voice. His Holy Spirit has been my teacher taking me from glory to glory.

But the Helper, the Holy Spirit, whom the Father will send in My name, He will teach you all things, and bring to your remembrance all things that I said to you. (John 14:26)

The focus of this book will be stories of my encounters as God revealed Himself. According to my experience, the evidence has been overwhelmingly of God's existence. There is not a physical being standing in front of us, therefore, it might cause one to feel uncertain of His existence. The problem with that is that God's ways are higher than our ways. It takes some acclimation and just like in any relationship; it takes a joint effort to communicate well. The Bible is very explicit how God communicates. As we draw near to God, He draws near to us (James 4:8). As I have come to know God, I have certainly found that He is who He says He is! The Bible is proof of His existence with countless stories being detailed through the eyes of people. As we read about their accounts it is exciting, but it is important that we experience God for ourselves. Hopefully, as you read this book you will recognize the evidence of His existence throughout your own life.

I am confident that the disciples were built up in great faith when Jesus began appearing to them after the resurrection. As Jesus died on the cross His people scattered in fear. When He began revealing Himself in the weeks following, it was all the evidence they needed to become stronger in faith and to become bona fide believers. Paul states that Jesus appeared to over five hundred people after the resurrection, launching great evidence to a multitude that He existed. (1Cor. 15:6)

I have been recording my experiences with the Lord for many years. If He spoke something, I wrote the words down. I valued the words He spoke, and I valued what the Lord showed me. I recorded nearly every dream and recorded countless visions. My whole life, as a Christian, was for a purpose of telling others about Him. I earnestly questioned where all these encounters would lead me. I initially thought it was just solely for me until I realized that I could not stop talking about the Lord and all He was doing. His desire is to have innumerable encounters with you and me. He wants you to know Him as the God He truly is and that will only come with communion with Him. I think He is truly unknown to most people. Just like me, I think people think they know God, but there is much more intimacy available. Actually, the more I learn about God makes me recognize there's much more to learn and to experience.

Then Paul stood in the midst of the Areopagus and said, "Men of Athens, I perceive that in all things you are very religious; for as I was passing through and considering the objects of your worship, I even found an altar with this inscription: TO THE UNKNOWN GOD. Therefore, the One whom you worship without knowing, Him I proclaim to you (Acts 17:22-23)

I have grown to know the Lord in ways I never knew were possible. I was not raised in church, so I did not know how to have a relationship with Jesus, nor did I have any preconceived expectations. Once I made the confession to believe and then to receive, He began revealing Himself to me. My life with the Lord became more exciting by the day, by the year, and here I am over thirty years later.

God has taught and shown me so much. I see it as being the most fulfilling life a person could possibly have. I am His child and He is my heavenly Father. As He has revealed His personality, His nature, His love, His concerns and His kingdom I have become completely devoted to Him.

In the beginning, I started having an avid prayer life. Of course, prayer is just talking to God, so I talked to Him night and day. He let me talk and talk and talk, then one day He let me know He had lots to say Himself!

I was beyond surprised!

In this book I will use the names, God, Jesus, and Holy Spirit interchangeably. As they are three in one, I will use each name at various times as I feel comfortable. I hope this does not confuse anyone. I know that some have a closer connection with Father God. Some people have a closer connection with Jesus. I first felt a closer connection with Jesus, but the more I read the Bible, the more I felt a closeness to God the Father. Jesus said, "If you know me you know the Father." I now have a direct relationship and a greater understanding of the work of the Holy Spirit. Hopefully, the readers will realize the importance of the third part of the Godhead (The Holy Spirit). He is vital and we must acknowledge Him equally for His work upon the earth today. Holy Spirit came because Jesus went to the Father and He plays a dynamic role in our lives. He is God's own Spirit and is sent to unite with God's people. He was specifically sent to do the works of the Father when Jesus left.

"If you had known Me, you would have known My Father also; and from now on you know Him and have seen Him."(John 14:7)

Nevertheless, I tell you the truth. It is to your advantage that I go away; for if I do not go away, the Helper will not come to you; but if I depart, I will send Him to you. (John 16:7)

I will do my best at telling the story of my life as He has directed me to do. I am just an average person, yet, I have encountered God throughout my Christian walk. I serve a Great God and He has woven great things into and throughout my life. He wants us to understand that He is the same in all our lives and it doesn't matter if we become great or not because He is GREAT in us! He wants to empower each of us, even with all our frailties, by filling us with the Holy Spirit.

Two weeks from my salvation experience I was filled with the Holy Spirit and began an empowered journey. I experienced a power come upon me that I could never deny nor forget. It was such a wonderful experience and I knew this was something not of a natural phenomenon. I knew it was supernatural! It was, at this time, when the Holy Spirit became my closest friend and teacher.

For our gospel did not come to you in word only, but also in power, and in the Holy Spirit and in much assurance, as you know what kind of men we were among you for your sake. (1Thes 1:5)

I lacked for nothing. I was given everything needed to begin this journey and now it was my turn to go forward as a born again, Holy Spirit filled child of God. What would I do with it all? I began praying in that heavenly language and in English for hours at a time. I read the Bible every chance I got. I couldn't get enough of **Him**. I was so grateful God took me out of a life that was dead and riddled with lies. As He brought me into truth, life became very interesting and exciting. I immediately recognized its genuine quality. It was real!!!

I see this book as a love story. It is a story how I fell deeply in love with a God that first loved me.

I was changed instantly and transformed slowly.

The Holy Spirit gave me a heart to pray for others and I began to hear the heart of God for the first time. The Lord moved me from one wonderful encounter to another and I grew spiritually. I experienced such joy! I stopped trying to fill the void inside and allowed God to fill me. I had complete fulfilment by reading, praying and getting to know the Father, the Son, and the Holy Spirit. I hope you enjoy reading this story as much as I have had living it.

CHAPTER 3

Evidence of A God When We Are Far From Him

But now, thus says the Lord, who created you, O Jacob, And He who formed you, O Israel: "Fear not, for I have redeemed you; I have called you by your name; You are Mine. When you pass through the waters, I will be with you; And through the rivers, they shall not overflow you. When you walk through the fire, you shall not be burned, Nor shall the flame scorch you. For I am the Lord your God, The Holy One of Israel, your Savior; (Is. 43:1-3)

I had a wonderful senior year in high school filled with lots of friends and fun. My best friend, Susie, and I were inseparable. I met Susie in my sophomore year, and we hit it off immediately. Being in a new school, we both encountered some challenges. We came up with a plan that changed our lives. To this day we think it was a plan that the Lord gave us. We decided that we would start smiling all the time. Both of us were a bit sad leaving our old schools so we thought that if we smiled all the time people would think we were happy. We thought that other people would want to be around us if they thought we were happy. Well, one thing led to another and silly as it may sound, it worked marvelously!

We had more friends than anyone could ever dream of and seemed to be living the high life. To this day we often laugh at our little plan way back then and always encourage each other, "Keep Smiling!" Truly, the smiling plan worked both ways. The more we smiled the happier we became.

At the end of our senior year, after graduation, we decided that we would go on a senior trip to Florida. We would use our graduation money to pay for the trip. Susie and I flew down to Daytona Beach and joined others from our graduating class. You can imagine what that was all about! The drinking age, at that time, was 18 in Florida. We were engaged in nights of partying and drinking. Thinking back, it was primarily good, clean fun except for the drinking. We managed to meet many nice people on our trip, except for the night we met the two morticians. They began telling graphic details of their job which freaked us out! We high tailed it out of that place, quick! As I remember, we laughed hysterically all the way back to our hotel.

The fun was winding down and it was our last day of the trip. We decided to take one last swim before boarding our flight for home. Susie was a certified lifeguard and I was a certified scuba diver, so swimming was what we did, and did it well. I never had a single thought of having any problems in the water.

We walked to the edge of the ocean and by the time we were knee deep we felt a real strong pull on our legs. We never thought much about it and we even laughed about it.

Little did we know this could have been our last swim!

We walked out a few feet further and shortly thereafter, found that the sand had disappeared from beneath us. As we were side by side, we kept swimming and swimming fighting to get back to get our footing in the sand. We were getting tired, quickly. As I said, we both were very strong swimmers, yet, here we were needing help. I realized rather quickly that this must be an undertow. I was always taught to dive deep and swim perpendicular to the current to get out of an undertow. So, I tried doing what I had been taught, but it didn't get me out of the strong current that continued to pull me out further into the ocean. Susie and I were getting farther and farther apart, and I became afraid.

I knew I was in trouble but felt too embarrassed to holler out for help. Within moments there were three little boys being drawn into the undertow along with us. We shouted to them to go back, but that was a waste of time, for they were pulled in just as quickly as we had been. The boys were very young and were between 6-9 years old. The youngest one latched on to me around the neck. The other two were swimming with Susie and were being drawn farther out into the ocean.

By now, I was physically exhausted. I told the boy to hold his breath and we were going under water to get out of the undertow. I made a weak attempt, but I couldn't swim very far before having to make it back up to the surface. It seemed so strange because people were everywhere. They were all around us, laughing and screaming and having the best time. Yet, here we were fighting for our lives.

I couldn't keep myself and the little boy above water any longer. I sunk down into the water and began to fight my way up and finally yelled help as loud as I could. No one seemed to notice us or hear us. Down I went again, and I feverishly fought my way back up again telling the little boy to kick. I knew we were drowning! For the third time, I sunk even deeper under the water and knew I wasn't going to be able to continue. On the third time coming up I yelled for help. A young man with dark hair, simply, reached in with his hand and pulled me to him. That's all it took, one pull to safety. He must have taken the little boy because I do not remember helping the little boy to the shore. All I was thinking was about my friend and saving her. She was so far out in the ocean that I could barely see her and the boys.

I moved limply and quickly as possible out of the water to the edge of the beach, all the while looking for Susie. I was so completely physically exhausted that I couldn't hardly breath or move. I felt like I was moving in slow motion. I began to scream and jump up and down and pointing to my friend way out in the ocean. I did not have the energy to remotely come close to the lifeguard's stand, so I just continued to scream and point toward Susie's direction. Remarkably, the lifeguard jumped off the stand and was running toward the water. I feared he would be too late. He began to swim in the direction of my friend with a floatation device. By this time, I was crying hysterically and feared she would drown. I literally was having flashes of me on the return flight, alone. I was horrified at the thought.

Susie was finally rescued, along with the boys, and thankfully so. I remembered thinking as I looked at the boy's father and how he had no idea how close we all came to be drowning. For the next few minutes Susie and I sat fearfully watching as they rescued several people in that very same area. An hour later they finally blocked the beach off from swimmers because of that dangerous undertow.

What a scary incident that could have turned out completely different. Once I became a Christian, I thought about the day I almost drown and am baffled why I never cried out to God. I never prayed, nor even thought one single solitary thing about God during the drowning episode. I was so far from Him at that time in my life, but He was right there.

I know the Lord saw me drowning that day and then rescued me through that young man. I was so far from God that it never occurred to me to pray for help. I am amazed that God was faithful to me even when I wasn't faithful to Him or was I even mindful of Him. I was His child because I had made a confession of faith at twelve years old. The confession was sure, but the commitment on my part was nonexistent. I am so dearly grateful that God was faithful to me and got me to safety. I am extremely grateful He saved my best friend and those three little boys. I have so much to be thankful for in my life and I owe it all to a God that is evident. He stays close to us even when we are far from Him.

> *Let your conduct be without covetousness; be content with*
> *such things as you have. For He Himself has said, "I will*
> *never leave you nor forsake you." (Heb. 13:5)*

CHAPTER 4

Evidence of the Power of Jesus Through the cross

For the message of the cross is foolishness to those who are perishing, but to us who are being saved it is the power of God. (1 Cor. 1:18)

I was twelve when a local church sent around a bus in my neighborhood to take people to church. A couple of men, who were on that bus, stopped at my house and invited me to go to Graceland Baptist Church. After approval from my mom they began to stop and pick me up every week to attend Sunday school and the church service. Several weeks later, during the church service, there was an invitation to come forward to receive Christ. It was then that I went forward and prayed to receive Jesus as my Lord and savior. Honestly, I really did not have a great understanding what it meant to make such a confession. Whether we understand it or not is not contingent on its power. There is such enormous supremacy through what Jesus did on the cross and it becomes powerfully evident in a person's life. As a twelve-year-old, all I knew was that it was a good thing to do. However, several months later I had an experience that I will never forget. In hindsight, it was definite evidence of a change in my heart.

That morning, as a young girl, I asked Jesus to come into my heart, confessed any sin in my life, and proclaimed that I believed He died on the cross for me and was raised to new life. At that point in my life I did not recall much difference in myself even though I assure you God was already working. I really liked going to church and began getting involved with various activities. I was young and lived a somewhat innocent life where one would not notice a big change that took place after receiving Christ.

That next summer I went on vacation with my family to Rhode Island to visit relatives. After visiting my uncle's family, the opportunity for me to stay another week was presented. What an adventure! I have four cousins and two of them were my age. This was going to be a great time! I had never been allowed to do something like this before and besides that, I was going to fly home alone. I was thirteen at the time and I had flown many times with my family, so I was familiar with the process.

During my visit my cousins and I decided to go to the brand-new release of "Jesus Christ Superstar". Even though I knew somewhat of what Jesus did, I really didn't have the complete picture or understanding of what He had done for mankind, or for me. Upon the completion of the movie, ending with the crucifixion of Jesus, I began crying. I began weeping, uncontrollably. It was such an emotional episode that my cousins practically had to carry me back to the car. I wondered why my cousins were not equally moved. I was always happy and rarely broke down crying, so I knew something monumental had just taken place.

It was the power of Jesus dying on the cross!

It was my first visual understanding of His dying on the cross. I realized, later in years, that this was huge evidence of His power! It was so powerful because it moved me to the core of my being. It touched my heart, deeply. It was something that just happened and was unexpected. For the first time I recognized the full impact of what Jesus did for me.

Unfortunately, the years ahead did not exemplify His power. My family did not attend church and eventually I quit going to church after middle school. I think if I had stayed in church things would have been different, but God has a plan and only He knows why we go through certain things. What is so remarkable is that He uses those experiences of our life. He uses them like steppingstones. Nothing goes to waste because God uses the negative experiences along with the positive ones.

*And we know that all things work together for good to those who love
God, to those who are the called according to His purpose. (Rom. 8:28)*

I entered into high school and began to drink and party quite a bit.
I began to start living a worldly life and had lots of friends. After that, I
went to college and continued the party life. After a year and a half, I quit
school, moved to California, and shortly thereafter got married. I partied
often, and began smoking marijuana on a regular basis. Within 2 years I
found myself divorced, with a daughter, and a lifestyle that soon would
spiral out of control.

After four years of spiraling out of control I was steeped in getting
drunk. I was in a real mess and got there in a brief period. In those days,
I was waiting tables at a restaurant and started up a friendship with a girl
named Renee. She began to tell me that I ought to watch this show called
the 700 Club because her mother watched it and was healed. I'm not sure
why I began watching, other than God was drawing me, because what
she told me wasn't specific to me. God knows what works for each of us!

Once I began to watch the show, I watched it daily. At the end of
the show I would pray the prayer to receive Christ, EVERY DAY! Again,
I did not have any understanding of what I was doing. I did not even
remember the confession I had made twelve years earlier. But again, I
began to witness the power of Jesus and the work on the cross. I began to
lose interest in going to my boyfriend's house. I would even drink a whole
bottle of wine and COULD NOT get drunk. I continued to smoke pot,
but I WAS NOT getting high! I did not realize what was happening to me.
I certainly was losing interest in that whole scene and found that nothing
was working as usual. I even had the strange desire to go to church.

It was the power of Christ through the cross!

As I said earlier, I had not been raised in a practicing Christian home,
but I had seen a change in my mom since she and dad started attending
church in recent months. During that time, I remember talking to her
on the phone one day and as soon as I got off the phone I turned to my
boyfriend and distinctly said, "I don't know what she's got but I want it!"

It's funny how we can spiritually discern something even if we don't even know what it is. The Holy Spirit reveals it to us!

I had not told anyone about praying with the 700 Club until my mother came over on a day I was having trouble starting my car. As we sat on the couch, my mother could see the turmoil I was going through and urged me to pray to receive Christ. I began to cry and told her I had been praying with the 700 Club for two weeks! She had me pray once again with her. She said that when you confess Him before men, that Jesus is Lord, it becomes powerful because He confesses you before the Father.

"Therefore, whoever confesses Me before men, him I will also confess before My Father who is in heaven. But whoever denies Me before men, him I will also deny before My Father who is in heaven. (Matthew 10:32-33).

Embarrassed to say, but, as soon as I finished praying with her, I looked up and said that I still wanted to get high. Being the understanding person, my mother began to tell me about using the name of Jesus to break the desire off me. I had errands to run that day and she told me to pray against that desire to get high, all day. So, as I ran errands that day, I commanded the desire to smoke pot to leave me many times. Every time I had the thought of getting high, I commanded the desire to go in the mighty name of Jesus.

Once I returned home, I promptly and excitedly ran into my apartment and dumped all the marijuana down the toilet. I scurried outside and threw away my bong and pipes I used to smoke pot into the apartment dumpster. That was the end of getting high! Here I had smoked pot for four years, and that day forward I completely stopped smoking pot and drinking alcohol. I was delivered completely! Not another thought of getting high or getting drunk! I had just encountered the REAL problem solver and encountered definite evidence He existed!

There is Power of Jesus through the cross!

His death and resurrection were for me to have NEW life! Again, the power showed up way before my mind did. It showed up in my life! This was profound evidence of power that Jesus had and power that came through His death and resurrection from the cross! It was specific evidence to me that I had just gotten ahold of something tangible! It was a power to overcome those things that were holding me down and those things that were bringing confusion in my life. I was experiencing a sudden transformation and people saw it. My friends, my activity and my language all changed quickly from that point forward.

Therefore, if anyone is in Christ, he is a new creation; old things have passed away; behold, all things have become new. (2 Cor.5:17)

I was twenty-four years old when I made that second confession. Thankfully, I never turned back because what He was giving me made me high on life! I was energized like never before! Astonishingly, He never let me go. As I had accepted Him at an earlier age, He held on to me and brought me back to Him. I believe He will do this for us all. I know so many people that received Christ at an early age and then fall away. I believe He will bring them back, too, unless they just completely reject Him. He is so patient and loves us so much that He will do anything to capture our heart! Thank you, Jesus, for dying in my place to give me the power to overcome.

CHAPTER 5

Evidence of the Power of His Name

Therefore God also has highly exalted Him and given Him the name which is above every name, that at the name of Jesus every knee should bow, of those in heaven, and of those on earth, and of those under the earth, and that every tongue should confess that Jesus Christ is Lord, to the glory of God the Father. (Phil 2:9-11)

Right after receiving Christ as the Lord of my life He began giving me dreams. They were dreams showing me the power of His name. There were many dreams where I would be in a situation and I would use the name of Jesus to resolve the attack.

In one dream, I saw this huge snake repeatedly rise on a road and I would shout, "In the name of Jesus!" and a car would run over the snake. Each time the snake rose up, the powerful words brought destruction to it. In another dream robbers came in my home and I just yelled, "You leave in the name of Jesus!" and they left. I dreamed this dream several times with variations. It always ended the same where the intruders left upon the commanding them to do so in the powerful name of Jesus. I often wondered if I was being prepared for such an event.

In the earlier years, I dreamed I was standing at the top of the stairs at the home where I was raised and heard many demons in the basement.

Every time I would shout, "In the name of Jesus!" the demons would scream and wail, then those demons would come closer to the stairs and all I had to do was speak in a normal voice, "In the name of Jesus!" and they would scream and shriek and fall back from the stairwell. It was so powerful. Finally, I began singing, "In the name of Jesus!" and it had the same powerful effect. Isn't that an amazing way to learn the power of His name? I believe the Lord was also showing me the persistence of the enemy and that I was going to have to be vigilant in the fight.

For our struggle is not against flesh and blood, but against the rulers, against the authorities, against the powers of this dark world and against the spiritual forces of evil in the heavenly realms Eph 6:12

I had a scary dream one time. I dreamed I was sleeping, and these long fingernails came up over my mattress. I knew it was the devil and I was really scared. Finally, I mouthed with a trembling and fearful voice, "In the name of Jesus." The fingernails retracted and I woke up. Again, He taught me such authoritative power by using His name! It's rather humorous to dream that you are sleeping, but not so funny to see the enemy trying to get you. Not only did I have a sudden awareness that I now had an enemy, but I had the way to overcome him. Jesus began teaching me His ways as soon as I became His child. These dreams helped me to be strong in spiritual warfare. I knew the effectiveness of prayer came through the power of the name of Jesus and wisdom from the Holy Spirit.

Once the Lord told me that all I have to do is whisper His name. That exemplifies the great power of His name. Demons cannot stand that name! As we take authority in our lives, we must remember to take that authority in the name of Jesus. So many people do not know that we have authority over the enemy. The authority desperately needs to be taught. The Church must not forget the authority in Christ Jesus and teach this next generation. The power has been given and we must not deny that power! We must exercise the authority given by Jesus. Increasingly, I see a generation overcome with issues, lacking self-control, and living defeated lives. There is an answer for these things. His name is Jesus and there is great power in His name.

But know this, that in the last days perilous times will come: For men will be lovers of themselves, lovers of money, boasters, proud, blasphemers, disobedient to parents, unthankful, unholy, unloving, unforgiving, slanderers, without self-control, brutal, despisers of good, traitors, headstrong, haughty, lovers of pleasure rather than lovers of God, having a form of godliness but denying its power. And from such people turn away!
2 Tim.1:3-5

When my daughter was young, she was deathly afraid of dogs. When she saw a dog, she would cry and literally climb up your leg to get away from it. Once the Lord taught me about the power of His name, I began to take authority over this fear of dogs. I commanded the spirit of fear of dogs to leave my daughter. I said it over and over for several weeks. Finally, she was no longer afraid of dogs. It was so evident that someone who knew her well commented, "What happened to Amy?" They noticed she was not afraid of a dog that approached us. I simply told them that I had commanded fear to leave in the name of Jesus and it did! They were very amazed.

Another time I, specifically, remember my daughter being afraid of the dark. It became quite an episode. If you have kids, you might know what I mean. I began coming against the fear very aggressively and immediately she calmed right down. I was completely amazed at the instantaneous calming of the fear. These things made a believer out of me! I have had to take authority over fear in my own life and I no longer have the fear I used to have.

We should know that we can, and must, take authority over the enemy in our lives. When our children are small, we as adults must take authority over the enemy for them. Then, teach them to use the name of Jesus and His word as they get older. There is such power that is needed to live a free and victorious life and it comes through the name of Jesus.

I taught my children to take authority the whole time they lived in my home growing up. Over the years I discovered that the teaching of taking authority was becoming weaker in the church. In some places it has become non-existent. People are fighting this spiritual battle through the flesh. I pray that the church begins to be aggressive, once again, in teaching spiritual warfare. We must fight for our children, spouses, and our marriages. We must fight for our leaders and for this nation.

Anytime we see activity around us that is not of a Godly nature, we can take authority over it. Many situations can arise and be of the flesh nature, but still be caused by demonic influence. When dealing with demonic activity we need to speak the authoritative words out loud. Remember, the words do not have to be shouted. A whisper is just as powerful. There is power in the name, not in how loud we say it. I truly love the name of Jesus and have seen great evidence of its power!

> *Therefore, God also has highly exalted Him and given Him the name, which is above every name, that at the name of Jesus every knee should bow, of those in heaven, and of those on earth, and of those under the earth, and that every tongue should confess that Jesus Christ is Lord, to the glory of God the Father. Phil 2:9-11*

There is power in Jesus' name, power by His Word and there is power through the blood. God has given us power through His Son. We receive all the benefits from Jesus' sacrifice on the cross.

Jesus took authority as He was being tested in the desert. Every time satan tried to get Jesus to respond to him He countered the enemy with the Word. There is nothing more powerful than using scriptures as we take our authority against the enemy! As we become lax in taking authority the enemy runs amuck. When Jesus left, He left us in charge. We must use the authority given to experience victory.

Once we recognize an attack of the enemy, we must begin taking authority immediately. The key is recognizing it. If I feel unusually sad, for no reason, I break that depression or sadness off. The Holy Spirit will give discernment as to what to pray. I know that if we let those things go, they become strongholds. When I minister to women, they recognize strongholds that they struggle with. I can pray for them and command those things to leave, but they must eventually say enough is enough and take authority themselves. I tell many about the power of His name.

If you are a believer, it is your right to use His name!

And Jesus came and spoke to them, saying, "All authority has been given to Me in heaven and on earth. Matthew 28:18

Then the seventy returned with joy, saying, "Lord, even the demons are subject to us in Your name." Luke 10:17

CHAPTER 6

Evidence God Sent His Spirit

"And being assembled together with them, He commanded them not to depart from Jerusalem, but to wait for the Promise of the Father, "which," He said, "you have heard from Me; for John truly baptized with water, but you shall be baptized with the Holy Spirit not many days from now." (Acts 1:4-5)

When I received Jesus as Lord and Savior, I was feeling higher than I had ever felt. The joy was quite exhilarating, and I knew I had found something worth living for. I began spending a lot more time with my mother and started going to a Southern Baptist Church. My mother also started taking me to her Bible study.

Bible study was held at my mom's best friend's house and I knew her well. There were about eight people there. I felt slightly nervous because I had never been to a Bible study and everything was so new. Little did I know that it was going to get a little strange for me. They all began to sing and praise God. During this time, they held up their hands in worship to God. All I could think was that *I definitely was not going to raise my hands*! During worship some were quietly speaking in their prayer language. That did not make me feel uncomfortable because I had previously heard my mother speaking in this kind of language while praying during an altar call. It was all new to me, but I did not comprehend why they were raising their hands.

Later that night, after we went home, mom told me to begin praying that God would fill me with His Holy Spirit. Honestly, I had never heard anything about the Holy Spirit, but I fully trusted my mother, so I began to pray for God to fill me with His Spirit. I prayed several times each day for God to fill me, not really knowing what to expect. At this point I had not even read the Bible, so I was very unknowledgeable. I was like those in the Bible where they claimed they had not heard anything about the Holy Spirit since they had believed.

"Did you receive the Holy Spirit when you believed?" So, they said to him, "We have not so much as heard whether there is a Holy Spirit." (Acts 19:2)

I was in a state of extreme excitement about the Lord. I was learning new things and realizing there truly was a God in Heaven. He had delivered me from drugs and alcohol and then He divinely delivered me from smoking cigarettes in just two short weeks. It was a whirlwind of enlightenment so whatever my mother told me to do I was doing.

The following week I went over to my parent's house to visit. Mom told me to come in her bedroom to look at some new clothes she had just bought. While I was in her bedroom, I told her I was having pain in my abdomen. I had had a spastic colon for a couple of years that had been diagnosed while I lived in California. She had me lie down on her bed so she could pray for me. As I laid down, she began to pray for my abdomen to be healed. While she was praying, I was praying quietly that God would fill me with His Holy Spirit. Later, my mother told me she was praying quietly for me to receive the Holy Spirit as well.

Suddenly, I began to shake all over and began to speak in this unknown language. It came out fluently and boldly. I was literally shocked! My body felt like a vibrating machine. The power of God was all over me and the feeling was amazing. I continued to shake and speak in tongues for two hours. I was moved to my core and realized that not only was there a God in Heaven, but now I knew there was a Holy Spirit. I didn't know anything about the Holy Spirit, but He was introducing Himself to me in a BIG way. It was a supernatural experience. I had only heard my mother whispering faintly in her Holy Spirit language so when the boldness of this language came forth from me it was beyond amazing. I was in awe of a God that would show Himself in this manner. It was thrilling to go from not really believing there was a God to meeting Jesus and then being filled with this powerful Holy Spirit.

Later that night, while still at my parents I could not wait to get home and try to speak in that language again. I was so stirred in my spirit! The next day, as soon as I got home, I began praying in that beautiful prayer language. Some may say I am silly, but I prayed in tongues in the mirror just to see the words coming out of my mouth. I felt like a little child that had been given a miraculous gift. The more I prayed the better I felt, and the power was obvious. I could hear that the words were not gibberish but were words of a real language or languages. The more I prayed the more the language seemed to change. Even though I did not know how to speak any other language I could hear the different sounds that were familiar. The more I prayed in my prayer language I would hear Spanish, then German and even Asian. I could hear distinct languages that I had heard at some point during my lifetime. It was incredible!!! I had prayed to receive the Holy Spirit, and this was evidence that I received. We all have a measure of the Holy Spirit once we receive Jesus, but this is a complete submersion.

for John baptized with water, but you will be baptized with the Holy Spirit not many days from now." (Acts 1:5)

By this time, I was devouring the Bible and learning about the God of the Bible. When I began to read about the disciples and how they all received the Holy Spirit, just like me, I could hardly contain myself. My mother used to say I was like a balloon flying in the sky because I was so high on what I was experiencing. Jesus is emphatic that He wants people to receive the Holy Spirit. He stated that it was a good thing that He go because He was sending the Holy Spirit. The Holy Spirit is a part of the Godhead and vital for our walk with Him.

I had come from a dark place in my life and seemed to have jumped across the ocean to a new and adventurous place. I was so full of expectation and faith at that point that I was ready for anything God wanted to do. This was my experience without exaggeration! Some people I talk to did not have this same excitement as I had during conversion. I think God knew I needed something quick and transforming and it worked! I ran with Him and I never looked back. There was nothing to go back to that was as amazing as the Lord. I will say, I have continued to stay charged up for thirty-four years and have loved every minute of it.

I ask people about their experience of being baptized in the Holy Spirit and I get a variety of stories. They are quite diverse! My mother was crying from watching a Christian television show and as she walked into her bedroom for a tissue, she raised her hands and suddenly began to speak in tongues. By the way, from the day I was Baptized in the Holy Spirit I never hesitated to raise <u>both</u> my hands.

Every cell in my body praised God!

I was at a conference once and I heard a story of a woman that lived outside the United States. The Lord spoke to her to come to that conference and she had no idea why. Once she arrived, she saw that God had a divine purpose for her to be there. As she attended the services, she heard people worshipping in all sorts of languages. It was not until then did she understand that the unknown language she had spoken for years was the language of the Holy Spirit. She had never met anyone that spoke in tongues before that conference.

From the day that I was Spirit-filled, my prayer life blossomed. I spent many hours praying in my prayer language and praying in English. I prayed in tongues and sang in tongues. I cried for people to get saved and spent hours experiencing the powerful presence of God. The tangible evidence that God sent His Holy Spirit caused me to be such a strong believer. There was never again a doubt about Christianity after receiving Christ followed by receiving His Spirit. It seemed to have set my belief in stone. I saw it as a piece of what was to come. It was that little drop of Heaven to show me that my experience was authentic.

In Him you also trusted, after you heard the word of truth, the gospel of your salvation; in whom also, having believed, you were sealed with the Holy Spirit of promise, who is the guarantee of our inheritance until the redemption of the purchased possession, to the praise of His glory.
(Eph 1:13-14)

It astounded me as I read in the Bible that this miraculous event of being filled with the Holy Spirit began over two thousand years ago on the Day of Pentecost. The Holy Spirit caused people to speak with boldness and glorify God. Many witnessed this initial outpouring. Paul established some rules concerning speaking in tongues in the church to bring order, but he made two bold statements concerning this beautiful gift from God. For one he said that we were not to forbid people to speak in tongues. He also established its importance by claiming that he prayed in tongues more than anyone else. Paul's ministry was empowered by the Holy Spirit.

"I thank my God I speak with tongues more than you all;" (1Cor. 14:18)

Over the years, I watched my mother pray for many people to be filled with the Holy Spirit. For those that think you do not have to speak in tongues, I agree. You don't! Although, I will say **you can,** and I encourage you to pray that you be filled with God's Holy Spirit and then pray to release the Holy Spirit's language. In all the years that my mother prayed for people to receive the Holy Spirit, all but one released a prayer language. I witnessed close to a hundred people receive the empowerment of the Holy Spirit under my mother's ministering. I often ministered alongside her as she prayed with people. We ministered well together. I, myself, have prayed with many children and quite a few women and all but one of them released a prayer language (tongues). The woman admitted that she was afraid of it. I say you can speak in tongues when you receive the infilling of the Holy Spirit because scripture supports it. I have witnessed it time and time again. My lifelong experience has witnessed that God gives the gift of the Holy Spirit if the person desires it.

I prayed for my grandma to be filled with the Holy Spirit and she prayed in tongues. She was so cute when she prayed. She loved Jesus so much and I cannot wait to see her again someday. She was 4 feet 8 inches tall and round all about. My brothers and I knew we had arrived when we could stand under grandma's outstretched arms. Of course, that happened around the age of eight. She once told me that she had heard that when a person dies they lose nine pounds. She used to giggle about being in Heaven and being a 9-pound spirit. I can hear her cute little chuckle to this day. And I can't wait to see my little 9-pound grandma dancing around in Heaven.

I once taught vacation Bible school to seven and eight-year old kids. At the end of the week several received Jesus as their Lord and Savior. Three of them received the Holy Spirit and released the language of the Holy Spirit. Many years later when I was leading a women's group at Aglow International a young man came up to me. He was in the worship group we had for the night. When he came up to me, he said, "I know you!" "You prayed for me to receive the Holy Spirit when I was a little boy!" I was excited to hear that and to see him serving the Lord.

The Lord has had me praying for children quite often. I found that they receive immediately. Being children, they do not have to work through doubt and unbelief. They believe and receive easily and yes; they all receive the Holy Spirit's language.

"And they were all filled with the Holy Spirit and began to speak with other tongues, as the Spirit was giving them utterance." (Acts 2:4)

When my mother passed away many people were at the funeral home. So many people came up to me and said how much they loved her. I was amazed at how many people told me that Mom had prayed for them to be filled with the Holy Spirit. What a blessing!

Years earlier I assisted my mother in a church where she was invited to teach about the Holy Spirit. At the end, she prayed for everyone in the church. Countless people were filled with the Holy Spirit and released the Holy Spirit's language. I was astounded at the teenagers that received the Holy Spirit that night. It made me cry every time seeing how blessed they were, remembering my own experience.

They were endued with the power Jesus promised!

I was privileged to be able to pray with a couple of women at work to receive the Holy Spirit. They had already received Christ years before. They too, received the Holy Spirit's language. My daughter's boyfriends never had a chance. As long as they were saved, I would tell them about the Holy Spirit. And yes, they too got filled with the Holy Spirit and released the language of God's Spirit. When a person receives Christ as Lord and Savior it is a perfect time to simultaneously lay hands on them and have them ask to be filled with the Holy Spirit.

The language of the Spirit can also be called a prayer language. It is a way the Holy Spirit can pray a perfect prayer through an imperfect person. We often do not know what to pray or even how to pray and this prayer effectiveness is God's gift. If He gave it, then how important can it be? I say…

"Extremely Important!"

It was so important that Jesus told the disciples to stay in Jerusalem until the Holy Spirit came. Jesus said that it was important for Him to leave but that the Holy Spirit would come in place of Him. Jesus wanted everyone to receive the gift of the Holy Spirit. He said it was an enduement of power.

And, behold, I send the promise of my Father upon you: but tarry ye in the city of Jerusalem, until ye be endued with power from on high. (Luke 24:49)

In Jude it says that as we pray in the Spirit that it builds us up in our MOST HOLY FAITH! I along with many others in the body of Christ are testimony to this. In 1 Cor. 14:4 it says that the person that speaks in tongues edifies himself. The Holy Spirit came for many reasons and it is crucial for us to be built up in our most holy faith and to be edified. To be edified is to be built up.

While I was a teacher, I always fantasized about the last day that I would teach. My fantasy was that I was going to pray with the whole class and have the children pray, if they wanted, to receive Jesus. Then I was going to pray for them to receive the Holy Spirit. It was very premeditated! I figured they couldn't do anything to me because it would be my last day. Besides that, I taught in the same school for my entire teaching career. It was home!

Well, after twenty-four years I was coming upon the day. The Big Day! Would I do what I had dreamed of all these years? I was down to the last hour of class with a precious bunch of first graders. I loved them so much! They were my last! I called them all to the carpet and started telling them how much I loved them and that I wanted to pray a blessing on them as they left my classroom. I started praying. I prayed for them to be safe and that they would have a good life and so on and so on. Then, I started laying my hands on several of them and prayed that they would receive Jesus and, simultaneously, I prayed that they would receive the Holy Spirit. When I finished everyone was very quiet. It was a sweet ending to twenty-four rewarding years of teaching. It was not quite as dramatic as I had envisioned, but it seemed very natural and was exactly how God wanted it. It was in love.

As they all lined up for the buses to be called one little boy started hanging on the door handle. He then started speaking in unrecognizable words (yet, very recognizable to me). With a giggle and a grin, I said directly to the little boy, "What was that?" And he said with a giggle and a grin, "I don't know." I was so blessed that God would show me that little tiny bit of evidence that He was faithful and that He sent the Holy Spirit for these little ones. All those years of fantasizing…

**and even though it wasn't exactly how I imagined;
it was perfect according to His plan.**

CHAPTER 7

Evidence That God Speaks

To him the doorkeeper opens, and the sheep hear his voice; and he calls his own sheep by name and leads them out. And when he brings out his own sheep, he goes before them; and the sheep follow him, for they know his voice. Yet they will by no means follow a stranger, but will flee from him, for they do not know the voice of strangers." (John 10:3-5)

If you read the Bible you clearly see scriptural references that God speaks to people. Many people understand that God can speak but wonder if He will speak to them or whether He speaks today. The list is plentiful of those that heard God speak in the Bible. There are, also, many references where people spoke by the unction of the Holy Spirit in the New and old Testament scriptures. Jesus also appeared and spoke to people after the resurrection. I realize this is a far stretch for some to have confidence of knowing God has spoken to them. On the other hand, there are numerous people who are confident God speaks to man and hear His voice for themselves. The Bible is full of examples of where God and the Holy Spirit communicated with man. God has communicated by His presence, His voice and by His word. He has also communicated through dreams and visions and through His prophets and angels. There is unsurmountable proof that God is a communicative God.

Recently, a talk show host considered it mental illness to hear God speak. Talking to God was just fine, but when you hear God speak to you it is mental illness. That statement infuriated many in the Christian community. The debate is certain as to whether God speaks to man or not and it depends on who you talk with that determines their philosophy. There has also been people that have committed heinous crimes after proclaiming that God told them to do it and it would certainly raise many questions. For those that are believers and those that believe the Bible must believe God speaks. To understand God's nature according to the Bible we should be able to establish discernment of whether it is God.

God Is Love!

I, myself, had no belief one way or another until I became a Christian. I began to see fulfillment after fulfillment of the Bible manifesting in my own life. After receiving Jesus and then getting filled with the Spirit I saw plainly where it was written in scripture. People, just like me, were being filled with the Holy Spirit in the book of Acts which was recorded over two thousand years ago. That was astonishing to me. It was hard to fathom something so unique occurring to me and then finding the same occurrence in the Bible. I remember being stunned as I read the book of Acts. From that point, I began to be open to any experience that was exemplified in the Bible. As I began to read the Bible and hear testimonies, I realized God spoke to people. Although I, personally, had not had a lot of experience of hearing God. Usually I had strong impressions or feelings of what I attributed to being God speaking. My earliest ways I heard God speak were through dreams. The plumb line for me to accept something was that it had to depict a God of love and had to line up with the Word of God.

By lining up with those two stipulations it enabled me to freely experience the one, true God. How saddened God must be when His people reject who He is and what He wants to do. We must allow the freedom to the Holy Spirit within us! Where there is freedom of the Holy Spirit there is liberty. Rather than having a dead, boring, mundane life of dry religion we can relish in richness, joy, and an abundant life. I assure you, if we allow the Holy Spirit to teach, lead, guide, and direct, we will have a greater feeling of contentment and fulfillment. There is so much freedom as we rely on the Holy Spirit instead of relying upon our own understanding. Holy Spirit knows all and will reveal to us what is needed for every situation. Unfortunately, greater revelation of the working of the Holy Spirit came later in my Christianity.

The story I am about to tell happened ten years after becoming a Christian. It is the most incredible turning point in my life. It truly transformed me in the way I viewed God and the way I responded to Him. I have told this story in each of my books because it made a profound change in my life. It continues to be that one encounter that began to drive my passion toward kingdom living, people serving, and God loving. I desire to return as much as I am able because God has given me so much! This book is in response to Him. My heart can only respond in one way to Him and with much delight.

I say, "Yes, Lord!"

I had taken my eldest daughter to church to board a bus for church camp. On the way home, I began praying in my prayer language and was talking to the Lord. I was praying intently and what you might say, rather fervently! Something began to happen that had never occurred before. While I was praying in tongues, I started to hear bits and pieces in English. The more I prayed, the more I heard it in English. I was extremely inquisitive because I had never heard my prayer language in English before. I valued speaking in tongues highly and had prayed hours upon hours allowing the Holy Spirit to pray through me. I knew it was the perfect way to pray, but I had never recognized hearing English words as I prayed in tongues. Although, scripture encourages us to pray that we may interpret tongues.

Therefore, let him who speaks in a tongue pray that he may interpret.
(1Cor 14:13)

This may be foreign to some of my readers, but I had been praying in tongues for **ten years,** so my thought was if I was hearing it in English for the first time God must want to reveal something to me. The more I drove around and prayed I heard specific things as if I were overhearing someone else in conversation. I heard the Holy Spirit speaking to someone through me. That someone I felt was an angel. Now, I know, this sounds a bit out there, but give me some time because this event opened the door to remarkable encounters with God in coming years.

In the beginning, I had to really focus to hear the English as I prayed in the Spirit. The more I focused, the clearer it became, and I could hear most of the conversation. I knew it was a conversation because I could hear one side. It was almost like when you are listening to someone talking on the phone and you cannot hear what the other person is saying. I did not hear what the angel was saying but was getting the idea of the conversation because what I was hearing the Holy Spirit say in English. I can't even tell you why I thought the Holy Spirit was talking to an angel except that I just felt that He was. The Holy Spirit spoke about some events that went on in a meeting and began talking about individual people. I thought this was very odd that I was hearing this conversation! This had never happened in my ten-year walk with the Lord and there must be something He wanted me to hear.

So, I continued to pray in the Holy Spirit's language, and I listened and listened. I continued to drive around all through an area of Floyds Knobs, Indiana. I noticed my gas gauge was on empty and so I stopped praying and spoke to the Lord and asked Him if I needed to get some gas. He stated clearly that I did not need to stop and get gas and detailed that we could ride on fumes. That gave me a chuckle and I proceeded out of an area called Highlander Point. Back in that time, there was only one gas station in the area and that was at Highlander Point. As I continued to listen once again to the English words of the Holy Spirit, I pulled up to the stop light where I was leaving the area. As soon as I did this, a thought ran through my mind. I was going to get out on one of these roads and run out of gas! Abruptly, the English words that I was hearing completely changed tone and direction. No longer was I listening to a conversation, but I heard the words directed toward me!

"Do you not know who you serve?"
Again, I heard sternly, "Do you not know who you serve?"
and for the third time,

"Do you not know who you serve?"

I literally thought I would fall over with shock. I thought my heart was going to pop out of my chest. From that point I heard those beautiful words in English describe Jesus. The Spirit of God began to talk about Jesus. His whole way of speaking changed from casual talk to such a seriousness and He spoke in such **Awe about Jesus.** He was now having a conversation with ME. He kept speaking about Jesus and how He was supreme. At this point, He had my complete undivided attention! I was in awe of all that was going on and in awe of all that I heard as the Holy Spirit spoke about Jesus.

"Howbeit when he, the Spirit of truth, is come, he will guide you into all truth: for he shall not speak of himself; but whatsoever he shall hear, that shall he speak: and he will shew you things to come." (John 16:13 KJV)

For the next half hour, the Holy Spirit spoke about Jesus and spoke direction for me in the coming days. As I continued throughout the night I heard more and more clearly. A real emphasis throughout the night was that He was going to finely tune me to hear His Voice. He said this over and over. He also told me to listen with my heart and not my mind. He spoke concerning various people in my life and about my family. The Holy Spirit spoke of the enemy's devises and to be very aware of the enemy's attacks. He kept repeatedly saying, "Use the name of Jesus!" He claimed, "All you have to do is *whisper* the name of Jesus!" I'll never forget how precisely He spoke those words. He also told me to come and sit with Him two times a week for two years and that He was going to teach me to hear His voice.

Then, as suddenly as God had begun speaking by the Holy Spirit, He was completely silent. Instantly, I knew He was finished talking. It was just totally quiet. There was such stillness, such peace. All that I had heard and experienced in that short 45-minute timeframe would change the rest of my life. It would send me on a course in life that was full of adventure. I had just experienced a 'suddenly' from God. I lingered in that peace for a few minutes as I sat in my car in my driveway. I was filled with zeal, with wonder, and then I ran inside and told my family what happened.

I do not know if my family really understood what had just occurred. My children were small back then. My husband listened and smiled as I recounted the event, I'm sure. I on the contrary, was jumping out of my skin! I was so enthralled in what had just happened and I did not want to forget a thing. So, I ran to the typewriter, sat down, and typed out the whole experience. This was assuredly only the beginning. It was at this point I began to record almost everything I possibly could pertaining to the Lord.

> *Thus speaks the Lord God of Israel, saying: 'Write in a book for yourself all the words that I have spoken to you. (Jer. 30:2)*

CHAPTER 8

Evidence That God Teaches by The Power of the Holy Spirit

But the Helper, the Holy Spirit, whom the Father will send in My name, He will teach you all things, and bring to your remembrance all things that I said to you. (John 14:26)

After that amazing experience when God spoke to me in my car I began to sit before Him on a regular basis. He had asked me to come and meet with Him twice a week. However, when I realized what was happening, I was deeply drawn into His plan of teaching me and I began to meet Him daily. Some days I sat before Him several times a day awaking early and staying up late just to hear His words. I wanted to know this God that was so personal. Once I heard His voice, I wanted to hear it more and more. As I heard God's words to me, I felt enriched and I was utterly intrigued.

I always thought I knew the Lord, but this was another level of relationship and I was very excited to see what this was all about! The Lord told me one time that I loved Him like a person who had a crush on someone. I read about God in the Bible and I had heard about God, but I did not truly know Him. Those words surprised me because I thought I had this great relationship with the Lord. I was doing a massive amount of talking to God but hearing from Him was far less. My relationship was rather one sided and selfish, yet I was walking in all that I knew to walk in. Little did I know that God was preparing to take me on a venture of a lifetime of hearing His voice. I was going to get to know God in a most unique way. Through this I was being completely fulfilled and being shown evidence that God speaks to His people by way of the Holy Spirit. I was going to truly get to know God, Jesus and Holy Spirit intimately.

Each time I would sit down and begin praying in tongues I would have pen and notebook in hand. In just a few seconds, I could hear English and I would begin writing the English words. This may sound strange, but this is how the Lord directed me. He was going to teach me to hear His voice and I wanted to hear it as clearly as I did in the car that first night. Just as sure as I heard His voice that night I, again, heard it each time I sat before Him and journaled. I heard the Holy Spirit's language turn into English, and I wrote all that I heard. The Lord began telling me stories that illustrated aspects of His kingdom principles. He used everyday items to illustrate ideas that He wanted to get across to me. It was incredibly engaging as I listened and learned all that the Holy Spirit imparted to me. I truly wish the Bible gave greater details of how people heard the Holy Spirit. Although, there are several scriptures that describe this occurrence. Philip heard the Spirit directing him to approach a man from Ethiopia. Because of Philip's obedience he was used to evangelize. The Eunuch received the message of the gospel and was baptized by Philip.

> *And sitting in his chariot (Eunuch from Ethiopia), he was reading Isaiah the prophet. Then, the Spirit said to Philip, "Go near and overtake this chariot. "So, Philip ran to him, and heard him reading the prophet Isaiah, and said, "Do you understand what you are reading?" And he said, "How can I, unless someone guides me?" And he asked Philip to come up and sit with him. (acts 8:28-31)*

At first, as I sat before the Lord, I struggled with many distractions. I would start looking around and start thinking about other things. I was very undisciplined. The Lord was so patient with me, and He always got my attention to refocus on Him. Once the Holy Spirit asked me how long I was going to look at this spot on the wall. How funny is that? It was important that I focus on Him and His words! The more I focused, the more clearly, I heard the English words. I was eager to hear every word. The words were filled with expression, reflection and showed me the Lords personality. I would pray in the Spirit and write quickly what I was hearing in English. The words I wrote were words of teaching, encouragement, and of direction for me and my life. Some of the words described future events. The words were so uplifting to me and I learned of God's character through the journaling. I began to understand what was important according to Him. I realized how much He cared for people because He talked about people a lot.

Over the first year the Lord told me over two hundred stories. They were like parables using common items as illustrations. The Holy Spirit also gave me short proverbial style tidbits. I wrote everything down and I am glad I did because the journals have been a great resource to remembering all that I heard. After the first year the Lord spoke to me to gather all the stories from the journals. I went back to the first year's journals and dogeared every story and tidbit of wisdom. There were thirteen journals from the first year. I typed them up and laid them around the living room floor. I remember being surprised by the number of stories I had. My next job was to place relatable scriptures to each story. The Lord showed me how to organize the compilation of stories and I created a booklet. Another year later the Lord spoke to me and gave me several titles to books. The first book was to be a study on the voice of God including my testimony. I completed it in six weeks and could feel the empowerment of the Holy Spirit. It was the first book that I published. I had no idea that the wonderful time I was sharing with the Lord would be shared with others. This was my private life getting to know my Jesus. It was not until the Lord began giving me these assignments did I realize He had a greater purpose for all that He was doing.

What was so amazing was in the journals there are no rewrites or changing of sentences in all 50 journals. Even after going to college and completing a master's degree in education, I have never been able to write papers without writing them over and over. Nor have I written anything without making many corrections. As I heard God's voice through the Holy Spirit and journaled His words, it helped the scripture come alive for me. Everything I heard and wrote became valuable to me and created an increase in my spiritual growth. It drew me ever so close and in love with Jesus. As I read the Bible it no longer was like reading stories. I could visualize Jesus saying the things He said. I felt like I was beginning to know the Lord personally by hearing His voice. I was getting to know His character and His heart's desire for people. I was interacting with a God of love, peace and of joy. Each time I would get up from my time with the Lord I would bubble all over with excitement and delight. It's hard to describe how thrilling it was to hear His voice and to learn so much. It continues to be this way, still, today!

Now hope does not disappoint, because the love of God has been poured out in our hearts by the Holy Spirit who was given to us. (Ro 5:5)

I realized that this practice was not commonplace and that initially concerned me. The more I read the Bible the more I found miraculous events such as my encounter and it alleviated me. I was growing in relationship with the Lord and being built up in such a way that the controversary no longer mattered. By entering into this covenant of communication my life became enriched in ways I never anticipated, and it was worth any debate. I frequently had my Mother read what I journaled. She encouraged me and felt confident that the words stayed in the parameters of scripture. I was gaining so much out of hearing His voice and have realized how valuable it is to hear.

The Lord told me I was operating in the Holy Spirit's gift of 'Interpretation of Tongues'. I thought this to be very interesting and it changed my understanding about that gift. I had always heard of that vocal gift occurring within a body of believers where one would speak in tongues and another would serve the interpretation. I do recall once in a while where one would speak publicly in tongues and then the same person interpreted in English. The practice was quite common in years past, but I rarely see this gift active in many of the churches I have attended in recent years. Sadly, people have pushed the Holy Spirit from the church service today and what we need most is…**The power the Holy Spirit provides.**

*He who speaks in a tongue **edifies** himself, but he who prophesies **edifies** the church. (1Cor 14:4)*

God has made it so easy to pray anywhere and at any time as we avail ourselves to the Holy Spirit. For me, praying in tongues comes out fluently as I pray back and forth from English to the language of the Holy Spirit. This is different from my time as I journal the words, as it is under the operation of Interpretation of tongues. In the realm of prayer, I experience increased power using tongues and English simultaneously and know that it is by the same Spirit in which I am receiving revelation. When we pray in this manner the English words prayed can be Holy Spirit led. That is one reason I encourage other intercessors to pray in the Spirit during intercessory prayer. Frequently, very unique prayers come forth that would not be characteristic of what our natural mind would pray. Revelatory praying is extremely imperative. At times, the Holy Spirit gives discernment how and where the enemy is operating. With this discernment we can counter the enemy's actions with words of life.

As I pray in the language of the Holy Spirit, I hear recognizable languages which sound familiar from different parts of the world. One time I had a Hispanic woman tell me I was speaking in Spanish. She said I was proclaiming healing for the woman I was praying for. Both her and her daughter stated they were hearing me in their language and seemed to get very excited about this. From that initial encounter in my car, I also began to have all kinds of visions, flashes of pictures. They were illustrations to what I was hearing, and they have been very enabling to pray effectively. You will hear much more about these encounters in later chapters.

I was quite amazed with the new and greater perimeter God was bringing me into. How could I pray in tongues and hear it in English? Only by the Holy Spirit could I do this. Only through the revelation of Christ was I able to trust in it. Many people might raise their eyebrows at such a possibility after hearing about my encounter. I would have questioned that myself before this happened to me because I had never heard of anyone hearing English while speaking in tongues. Since then, I heard a well-known preacher claim as he prayed in tongues that it came back to him in English. I have also heard a couple other testimonies where people received interpretation of tongues while praying. Either it's rare or people just don't talk about it. We all can pray to interpret.

> *For this reason, the one who speaks in a tongue should pray*
> *that they may interpret what they say. (1Cor 14:13)*

I have always realized that the Holy Spirit's language must be extremely important or why would the Lord give it to people! I always esteemed it highly because it was a gift from the Lord. Why did Jesus tell His disciples to stay in Jerusalem until the Holy Spirit came? It was the last thing Jesus told people to do…Receive the Holy Spirit! It was vitally important, and He claimed it would fill them with power (Luke 24:49). I felt that definite importance of the Holy Language the day I received the Holy Spirit. I felt such physical power at first, then as I exercised in praying in tongues…

I experienced spiritual power.

> *Behold, I send the Promise of My Father upon you; but tarry in the city of*
> *Jerusalem until you are endued with power from on high." Luke 24:49*

The Word says that we will build ourselves up in our most holy faith as we pray in the Spirit (Jude 1:20). Paul said he prayed in tongues more than anyone else (1 Cor. 14:18). These reasons made me pray countless hours in my prayer language. I call it a prayer language because that defines it clearly for me. I use it to pray the perfect prayer of God! If Paul spoke in tongues more than anyone, then I assumed that I should also. I prayed for hours at a time using my prayer language and experienced the power and presence of God. I encourage anyone that has received the language of the Holy Spirit to use it extensively! If you lack power, pray in the Spirit and pray in the understanding. If anyone has not received this evidence of power, pray to be filled with His Spirit. He is faithful to give you what you need. The Holy Spirit is our comforter, helper, and teacher.

> *As they ministered to the Lord and fasted, the Holy Spirit*
> *said, "Now separate to Me Barnabas and Saul for the*
> *work to which I have called them." Acts 13:2*

It was ten years that I had faithfully prayed in the Spirit and I had never heard it in English until that day in the car. I realized I had a new revelation of God and I was ecstatic about this new revelation. I already had such love for the Lord, and this intensified that love. It was evident, to me, from the beginning that Jesus wanted more for His people. He relentlessly conveyed His love for the body of Christ and for the body to walk in greater potential. Jesus, by His Holy Spirit, helped me to understand these concepts and imparted to me this same desire for the body of Christ.

> *Most assuredly, I say to you, he who believes in Me, the*
> *works that I do he will do also; and greater works than these*
> *he will do, because I go to My Father. John 14:12*

After several months had passed, I was sitting watching the series "Matthew" on VHS. It centered on the book of Matthew from the Bible and reenacted everything Jesus said and did. I had read the Bible for years and definitely had read the book of Matthew many times. While I was watching this reenactment, I became dumbfounded. My jaw dropped with astonishment. I had the sudden realization that this was Jesus' teaching style to tell stories. I was flabbergasted! Throughout that movie, Jesus told story after story. This was the same Jesus that was speaking to me, teaching me, telling me stories. He was teaching the same way using objects and giving illustrations so that people could understand. He was teaching me by the Holy Spirit in like manner. The only difference was that I saw the objects in vision form.

What a Mighty God we serve!

It took me awhile to put all the pieces together trying to figure out all that He was doing. I am still trying to figure out the full picture and reason for all this! I realize now that my experience is not solely for me to enjoy, but to share with others. It gives hope in knowing our relationship can be tangible, one that can be real having aspects that are relatable. Jesus wants us all to know there can be more to having a relationship with Him, other than just knowing He exists. He wants us to experience His existence. I do know that He has been the greatest at teaching and revealing Himself to me and He will do the same for you.

As the years went by, I listened to God's words and dug into the Bible for words of truth as I felt myself being transformed. I diligently sought out Jesus, God, and the Holy Spirit through the Word and became very aware of them, the Godhead, the three in one. As God taught me by the Holy Spirit, He challenged me to be a better wife, mother and person. During all these years Jesus taught me about love by directing me with His love. He spoke correction at times too, but He always showed me a better way in the process. He inspired me to pray for others and to lean upon the understanding of His Holy Spirit rather than on my own understanding. He showed me evidence that He is alive, He speaks to His people and He cares deeply for us. He showed me evidence that He is the same yesterday, today, and forever.

Let your conduct be without covetousness; be content with such things as you have. For He Himself has said, "I will never leave you nor forsake you." So, we may boldly say: "The Lord is my helper; I will not fear. What can man do to me?" Remember those who rule over you, who have spoken the word of God to you, whose faith follow, considering the outcome of their conduct. Jesus Christ is the same yesterday, today, and forever.
(Heb 13:5-8)

Here are 50 things the Holy Spirit does according to the New Testament.

1. The Spirit convicts the world of sin, righteousness, and judgment (John 16:8).
2. The Spirit guides us into all truth (John 16:13).
3. The Spirit regenerates us (John 3:5-8; Titus 3:5).
4. The Spirit glorifies and testifies of Christ (John 15:26; 16:14).
5. The Spirit reveals Christ to us and in us (John 16:14-15).
6. The Spirit leads us (Rom. 8:14; Gal. 5:18; Matt. 4:1; Luke 4:1).
7. The Spirit sanctifies us (2 Thess. 2:13; 1 Pet. 1:2; Rom. 5:16).
8. The Spirit empowers us (Luke 4:14; 24:49; Rom. 15:19; Acts 1:8).
9. The Spirit fills us (Eph. 5:18; Acts 2:4; 4:8, 31; 9:17).
10. The Spirit teaches us to pray (Rom. 8:26-27; Jude 1:20).
11. The Spirit bears witness in us that we are children of God (Rom. 8:16).

12. The Spirit produces in us the fruit or evidence of His work and presence (Gal. 5:22-23).
13. The Spirit distributes spiritual gifts and manifestations (the outshining) of His presence to and through the body (1 Cor. 12:4, 8-10; Heb. 2:4).
14. The Spirit anoints us for ministry (Luke 4:18; Acts 10:38).
15. The Spirit washes and renews us (Titus 3:5).
16. The Spirit brings unity and oneness to the body (Eph. 4:3; 2:14-18).
17. The Spirit is our guarantee and deposit of the future resurrection (2 Cor. 1:22; 2 Cor. 5:5).
18. The Spirit seals us unto the day of redemption (Eph. 1:13; 4:30).
19. The Spirit sets us free from the law of sin and death (Rom. 8:2).
20. The Spirit quickens our mortal bodies (Rom. 8:11).
21. The Spirit reveals the deep things of God to us (1 Cor. 2:10).
22. The Spirit reveals what has been given to us from God (1 Cor. 2:12).
23. The Spirit dwells in us (Rom. 8:9; 1 Cor. 3:16; 2 Tim. 1:14; John 14:17).
24. The Spirit speaks to, in, and through us (1 Cor. 12:3; 1 Tim. 4:1; Rev. 2:11; Heb 3:7; Matt. 10:20; Acts 2:4; 8:29; 10:19; 11:12, 28; 13:2; 16:6,7; 21:4,11).
25. The Spirit is the agent by which we are baptized into the body of Christ (1 Cor. 12:13).
26. The Spirit brings liberty (2 Cor. 3:17).
27. The Spirit transforms us into the image of Christ (2 Cor. 3:18).
28. The Spirit cries in our hearts, "Abba, Father" (Gal. 4:6).
29. The Spirit enables us to wait (Gal. 5:5).
30. The Spirit supplies us with Christ (Phil. 1:19, KJV).
31. The Spirit grants everlasting life (Gal. 6:8).
32. The Spirit gives us access to God the Father (Eph. 2:18).
33. The Spirit makes us (corporately) God's habitation (Eph. 2:22).
34. The Spirit reveals the mystery of God to us (Eph. 3:5).
35. The Spirit strengthens our spirits (Eph. 3:16).
36. The Spirit enables us to obey the truth (1 Pet. 1:22).
37. The Spirit enables us to know that Jesus abides in us (1 John 3:24; 4:13).

38. The Spirit confesses that Jesus came in the flesh (1John 4:2).
39. The Spirit says "Come, Lord Jesus" along with the bride (Rev. 22:17).
40. The Spirit dispenses God's love into our hearts (Rom. 5:5).
41. The Spirit bears witness to the truth in our conscience (Rom. 9:1).
42. The Spirit teaches us (1 Cor. 2:13; John 14:26).
43. The Spirit gives us joy (1 Thess. 1:6).
44. The Spirit enables some to preach the gospel (1 Pet. 1:12).
45. The Spirit moves us (2 Pet. 1:21).
46. The Spirit knows the things of God (1 Cor. 2:11).
47. The Spirit casts out demons (Matt. 12:28).
48. The Spirit brings things to our remembrance (John 14:26).
49. The Spirit comforts us (Acts 9:31).
50. The Spirit makes some overseers in the church and sends some out to the work of church planting [through the body] (Acts 20:28; 13:2).

CHAPTER 9

Evidence Jesus is
a Storyteller

*Another parable He spoke to them: "The kingdom of heaven is like
leaven, which a woman took and hid in three measures of meal till it was
all leavened." All these things Jesus spoke to the multitude in parables;
and without a parable He did not speak to them, (Matt. 13:33-34)*

Jesus was well known as s storyteller. He was a great communicator and
used parables to tell stories illustrating His Kingdom and His kingdom
principles. A parable can be a story using physical items to explain spiritual
principles. Parables also compare earthly truths with heavenly truths. Jesus
knew how to engage the listener using parables in His teaching. By doing
so He gave people great visualization which enhanced their understanding.
Biblically, Jesus used the illustrated stories to clearly describe and explain
as He taught. These comparisons to everyday life and items gave people
something to relate to as Jesus taught His truths. The Word says God's
ways are higher than our ways and therefore, He helps us understand on
our level. He told stories illustrated by using items that were common
in that day. He used agriculture, animal and plant life, clothing items,
kitchen items, etc. He astounded people by the wisdom as He related one
thing to another. He taught me in this same manner and astounded me
also.

When I began journaling, years ago, the Lord told me so many stories and I saw visions as He illustrated each one. Oddly, I wondered why He was telling me all these stories. As I stated earlier, it was not until I was watching the movie called "Matthew" did I realize that this was Jesus' style of teaching. The epiphany was overwhelming.

I learned rather quickly as the Lord illustrated His stories and made many comparisons while He was teaching me to hear His voice. I would have eventually learned all that the Lord wanted me to know by reading the Bible, but I learned expediently by listening to Him through the Holy Spirit. The Lord used many objects I was familiar with to illustrate His stories to me. God's Word was going deep into my spirit and it marked me for life for His purpose because of the way He used comparisons to explain His truths. Like Jesus' disciples, they were willing to die for their belief because they knew Him. Even after He was resurrected from the grave He came back and encountered not only the disciples, but others as He continued to teach them. Everything Jesus did built them up into great faith. That is why people were willing to die for their belief. They definitely knew who Jesus was, and they had such a revelation of the message He was conveying. Jesus built such trust because all that He spoke manifested. Often, they did not completely understand, yet they witnessed enough to believe. I, personally, have been witness to Jesus and His ways. My faith is strong and my belief of the validity of His word is very solid. Jesus reveals Himself to each of us uniquely. He builds us up in faith in diverse ways. He is creative and establishes relationship with each of us individually.

In this section I have written stories that the Holy Spirit imparted to me as Jesus taught me. I delighted in all His words and learned so much. I hope you enjoy these stories as well. They are copied straight from my journals. Recently, I stacked the journals on a table, and I measured them. The Lord told me that one day I would be able to stack the journals on top of my head and they would reach the ceiling. That made me laugh when He said that and after measuring them, I'd say they truly will reach the ceiling. A few years back, I almost burned all the journals. They were for me and my walk with the Lord and I did not want them to get in the wrong hands. The Lord spoke sternly to me as I contemplated on burning them. He spoke loud and clear, "Don't burn your bridges!" I felt the importance of His words and therefore did not burn them. I see, even now, a greater purpose to not destroy them as I am writing this book.

I have titled the stories for easy location. During each story the Lord gives me a vision or visions and then makes a statement of truth. There is always something I learned from each illustration and story.

In this first story the Lord illustrates the difference between His ways and our ways.

Holiness

Vision-I saw a woman washing an item of clothing on her washboard

A washtub! A woman may wash her clothing on the scrub board. (I saw an old-time scrubbing board) She scrubs, and she scrubs. Oh, finally she spies a hole in the article of clothing. Afterward, she determines that this article of clothing is worn out. It's been cleaned and cleaned. Finally, it comes to the end of the line of its use, but I say that my people are not like this. I clean, and I clean and see there are no holes, but when I clean there is righteousness. When I clean a holiness comes. YES, YES, see there is a holiness that comes. This holiness is not because of its worn-out state but because it is being prepared for its further use.

> *Pursue peace with all people, and holiness, without*
> *which no one will see the Lord: (Heb 12:14)*

It is interesting how Jesus uses a play on the word holiness. It made me laugh when He began to explain His process of cleansing and that it didn't cause holes. As He transitioned to discussing holiness I was surprised. The playfulness of His words delighted me.

Some of my favorite stories are the ones where the Lord uses humorous illustrations. Teaching using humor helps truth become more palatable. Jesus uses amusing illustrations such as in Matthew 23:24 when He describes the Scribes and Pharisees as being blind guides that would strain out a gnat yet swallow a camel. That statement had to cause people to chuckle and surely gave a definite picture of the state of the people according to Jesus.

When Your Flicker is Gone

*Vision-I saw a little candle standing alone

There was this little light. It flickered day and night and then it went out. It looked around and saw darkness. It strained to be lit again. It jumped up and down to create the light it once was. It just wasn't there. Then, all of a sudden, there came a knock at the door. It walked over and opened the door from which the knock came. When it opened the door, there stood a stranger. The stranger said, "How are you?" The light said, "Well I'm having trouble." The stranger said, "Well, how can I help?" The light said, "You can't help, there is nothing you can do." So, the stranger went away. Then came another knock at the door. This knock was a long, slow knock. The light decided not to answer this time.

Then the Lord said…

I have been calling you and you have not come to the door of opportunity. I have been knocking and you have not answered. I have sent others and you will not receive from them.

In this story I saw a little candle. This little candle was so cute, but as I watched this story play out, I became saddened. It is a shame the candle did not recognize its source of rescue! Sometimes we look past all the ways the Lord sends us for help. Either we do not recognize His intervention, or we are too stubborn to ask for help. Both ways end the same for the person. People stay in bad situations and live defeated lives while continuing in darkness.

Some stories the Lord spoke to me were extremely humorous. I laughed so hard as I listened and watched. As I wrote, sometimes, I could barely continue writing because of laughing. Jesus can be very witty. Even as I pray, the Lord gives me funny illustrations to exemplify the situation and I pray according to that illustration. He often uses a play on words just like in this story. I do not think people realize how humorous He can be.

I know I did not until He began using humor as He taught me. I'll never forget when the Lord showed me this clown. Most of all I will never forget the message that went with it.

Missing the Mark

Vision-I saw this clown putting on his makeup

There was this clown. He was putting on his makeup. As he was trying to put the makeup upon his lips, he kept missing. His makeup slid up his face and then it slid down his neck.

I heard the Lord laugh and say, "It really isn't this bad!"

Now the clown was very frustrated and wondered why he kept missing his mark. He tried very hard and each time he would miss his mark.

This is so like My people. Do you want to know why? My people keep trying to hit their mark. I say, they never will. It is comical for them to think they will, but I will take their hand and with My guidance they will truly go the right way. They are going to miss their mark many times but with Me, they will have the right makeup!

We are not perfect, and we continually fall short. Jesus wants us to know that it is alright because He is right there to help us. He is right there to guide us into all truth if we are willing. Jesus let me hear Him laugh during this story. He began to reveal His personality in this remarkable way. Jesus uses a play on the word makeup. The illustration is using makeup as a cosmetic that you place on your face. Then, in the end He turns the makeup as meaning the parts that we are composed of. I have such fond memories of Jesus telling me stories.

In this next story Jesus uses everyday common items and uses a familiar sight as an example of how we can become. I always love how Jesus teaches me that no matter what state we find ourselves in that He is able to bring us out of it.

Just A Little Bit of Jelly

Vision-I saw this clump of dried up jelly lying on a kitchen countertop along with the jar and a spoon.

There was just a little bit of jelly. It lay upon the counter. It blamed the spoon for its mishap. As it lay there blaming the spoon it began to dry up. It became hard and not supple as it had been created. Then, along came a dishrag and gave it relief. As the dishrag smoothed over the jelly it once again was supple. It arose out of its hardened state and rejoiced for the dishrag had brought it back to life again.

So, it is like unto My people. I shall smooth over them the moisture that is needed and once again they shall be renewed. They shall be sweet like unto jelly. But most of all, they shall be lifted.

In our lives many life-experiences can cause us to harden our hearts. Often, we go around blaming others and making excuses for our hardness or bitterness. Jesus knows exactly how to help us. His Word is like water as it washes over us, refreshing us. The water of the Word renews our mind and cleanses us. Only Jesus can truly be the lifter of our head. He can truly lift us from that hardened state. I think it is very interesting how Jesus describes Himself in this story as a wet dishrag. That does not sound too flattering yet think how this item is used as a perfect example of how Jesus humbled Himself to be the servant of all.

This next story Jesus uses an eagle along with other smaller birds to illustrate His message. Jesus, described as the powerful eagle, is being watched by many of us. I saw many birds symbolizing God's people. They were watching Jesus ever so intently with great expectation. As Jesus spoke this story to me, I could hear a tremendous screech echoing through the mountains which immediately got all the other bird's attention. This story was extremely vivid as this drama played out.

His Flock Will Meet Him in The Air

There was this great bird. He was bestowed with much strength and was a very powerful bird. He swooped down out of the sky with greatness. He passed many on his flight. Many gazed at him with an expectancy. They waited for him to notice them for when he saw them, he would do great things. He would land on tall mountains. He would fly with a swiftness that no other bird could fly.

But, unlike other birds, he had a screech that all would hear.

(I then heard a loud screech as of an eagle making his call)

When he screeched, all upon the ground heard. When they heard Him, they joined him in the sky. They then knew they were His! They knew that they were a part of Him and were on the same flight with Him. When they met Him in the sky, they then knew that they too possessed the same power that this great bird possessed. They too soared to great heights. They too knew that they belonged to this flock!! They went to great heights with this great bird. He took them to places they had never been and had never seen. He amazed them with the things that he showed them.

Then Jesus spoke to me and emphatically said, "So, I tell you, that these days that you stand and watch the works of the Lord, you too will be a part of these great things that He has created."

(Then I had the most awesome awareness that the things he had to show us after we are taken from this world would be beyond our wildest imaginations)

I am looking forward to viewing all that Jesus will show us as we join Him throughout eternity. We not only will be observers but will also be partakers of His world. It will be incredible to witness all of God's creation. As we follow Him in this life, we are able to move in His likeness. We can journey to great heights right here on earth as we are led by the Holy Spirit. It will forever increase once we leave the limitations of this natural physical body. Even now, as we are witness to Jesus' great works, we are eager to join Him in eternity.

But as it is written: "Eye has not seen, nor ear heard, nor have entered into the heart of man the things which God has prepared for those who love Him." But God has revealed them to us through His Spirit. For the Spirit searches all things, yes, the deep things of God. (1 Cor 2:9-10)

The Body

It's alive! It's alive and well on planet earth. It causes turmoil. It causes much trouble. It is a spirit that runs rampant upon the earth. It is a spirit of confusion. It must be bound. Bind confusion in the body of Christ.

The hand thinks it's supposed to slap the face. The foot thinks it's supposed to kick up dirt. The nose thinks it's supposed to smell for trouble. These things are all wrong. All the body parts are in the wrong place, doing all the wrong things. (Then I saw a human body and all the body parts fly off into all directions)

(Then, the Lord proceeded to say)

I am going to take each part and talk to them. When I send them back to the body, they will begin doing their proper job. They will have new insight and new direction. The hands will come together and work together. The feet will walk in unison. The ears will listen together, and the mouths will take turns to speak. The eyes will watch together. They will keep track of all the other working parts. The heads will organize. They will join together with ideas that I have planted within. The knees will join together in prayer and intercession. The elbows will join together and produce much work. The hearts will hear the voice of God and pump the messages to the rest of the body. I will, then, lay the body down and give her dreams. I will provide healing in every part of the body. When she rises up, she will feel good. She will feel organized. She will feel unified. She will be in one mind and one accord. She then will walk upright and holy. She, then, will walk the path of righteousness. She will then grab the people by the wayside, and they will join her. The people by the wayside will desire to walk in unity with her because of Me.

For God is not the author of confusion, but of peace,
as in all churches of the saints. 1 Cor 14:33

For as the body is one, and hath many members, and all the members of
that one body, being many, are one body: so also, is Christ. 1 Cor 12:12

This story about the body was a great source for prayer. I used its elements to pray intently for the body of Christ. Not only was it a great illustration of the body of Christ as God was seeing it, but it helped me to understand how intricately the body of Christ needed to work together. It also illustrated to me that every part of the body had great purpose. It also helped me to recognize the value of each person in the body. Many stories the Lord told me helped me to realize how deeply He cared for His people. His love and care transferred to me concerning the body of Christ because of His love and His earnest concern.

The Fisherman

Vision- I saw an old fisherman at a big lake

There was a worn-out old fisherman. He was very old. He looked a ripe age of 80. He continued to be faithful in his fishing. Year after year, he carried his rod and his tackle. Now, he was out one day at dusk. The lightning struck the water and gave him a great fright. All of a sudden, the fish began to float to the top, one by one. He ran around and scooped them up and put them on the small amount of ice. That night when he went home, he carried a large amount of fish to his wife. The old woman looked in surprise. She said, "Such an old man to catch so many fish." He said, "I carried on as usual and then, all of a sudden, there was a loud sound as a clap of thunder!" "Then, all around me was the catch of all catches, too numerous to bring home." "So, this is the story of my day."

But I say, as the Lord of all, "There will come a day that my voice will call out and the catch of the day will be quite numerous for I will call many to the surface."

In this story the fisherman symbolizes someone that has been in the ministry a long time being faithful to the great commission of bringing people to the knowledge of Christ. We are referred to as fisher of men according to Jesus. The thunder represents God's voice and the fish responded to its power. The wife symbolizes the Church witnessing a great incoming of salvations like she's never seen before. This is a prophetic story about the coming harvest during the end times. I think we are beginning to witness this great influx of salvations now but believe it will intensify in coming years.

The Lord presents Himself in the thunder and lightning on Mount Sinai in the old testament. God's presence resided on Mount Sinai and became a meeting place with Moses. God made himself known and heard from this place.

On the morning of the third day there was thunder and lightning,
with a thick cloud over the mountain, and a very loud trumpet
blast. Everyone in the camp trembled. Exod. 19:16

Move in Unity

An inchworm- It takes a very long time to reach its destination, not only because of its size but because of its motion. The front part of its body moves and then brings the back part of its body to meet up with the rest of the body. This method takes twice as long. This is like the body of Christ. See how half is in one place and the other half has to catch up?

until we all reach unity in the faith and in the knowledge
of the Son of God and become mature, attaining to the
whole measure of the fullness of Christ. (Eph 4:13)

Again, this story also gave me a source in which to pray for the body of Christ. As we observe throughout the earth the body of Christ does seem to be disjointed. One part of the body seems to be in one place and the other part of the body appears to be somewhere else. We only see a minute sector of the body, whereas, God sees on a larger scale and sees greater purposes of the body of Christ. Every believer moves along in faith on so many different levels and in such variance of pace. It is incredible how God keeps up with individuals and with specific sectors of the body.

This story broke my heart and is one for the born-again believer. To this day I cannot read it without crying. So often we do not go back to tell them!

You Must Go Back to Tell Them

There was this little boy. He was lost from his mother. So, he went up to many people and said, "Do you know where my mother went?" Of course, their answer was no, for they did not even know his mother. He dropped his head and said, "No one knows my mother and therefore does not even know where I can find her." Then the little boy looked up and there, all of a sudden, was his mother. He ran up to her. Then he ran back to all the people and said,

"See, this is my mother!" "See what she looks like?" "Isn't she nice?"

(Then the Lord said)

This is like you. When you are seeking me, you might ask others of me. But when you find me you must go back and show them me! You <u>must go back</u> and tell them of me!

In this story the mother symbolizes Jesus. Jesus is always there waiting to be discovered. As people, we always recognize our need for Jesus, yet sometimes it takes a while to find Him. We always recognize that something is missing without Him. Once we are reconciled to Christ, we must introduce others to Him. Thankfully, He first loved us. Thankfully He chose us! We must go back and introduce Jesus to those lost without Him.

Under Foot

Vision- I saw these three quarters pop out of a pocket one at a time

Three quarters fell out of a person's pocket. They began rolling. One rolled into a sewer. One rolled under a car. One rolled under a man's foot. Now which quarter do you think is in a safer place? For the one in the sewer is in the most disgusting place, one might say. The one under the car is in the most dangerous place. And the one under the foot is in the safest and the cleanest place. I say that this is not the case for the enemy. For he is under foot. He has chosen the other places, but I have chosen this place for him.

I understood the quarters falling out of the pocket to mean the enemy being kicked out of heaven. This was a unique way of describing where God has placed our enemy. God's ways are much higher than our ways. As we walk with the Lord and learn His ways, we gain understanding and wisdom.

And He said to them, "I saw Satan fall like lightning from heaven.

Behold, I give you the authority to trample on serpents and scorpions, and over all the power of the enemy, and nothing shall by any means hurt you. (Luke 10:18-19)

And the God of peace shall bruise Satan under your feet shortly. The grace of our Lord Jesus Christ be with you. Amen. Rom 16:20

Remove the Hat

Vision- I saw this black top hat on top of a person's head

This story is about a hat. The hat is worn on top. It is worn above the head. But no man is above the head. The hat therefore does not represent the man. This is where the enemy sets himself up, above the head. But see how easily the hat is removed?

(Then I saw a hand simply knock off the hat that was on top of the head)

Remove the hat that has set itself above the head. The word of God will do this.

Jesus fought against the enemy with the Word of God and this is just what we should do whenever he tries to exalt himself over the knowledge of God. God's people must take authority over the enemy. The power is in our hands.

For the weapons of our warfare are not carnal, but mighty through God to the pulling down of strong holds; casting down arguments and every high thing that exalts itself against the knowledge of God, bringing every thought into captivity to the obedience of Christ, (2 Cor 10:4-5)

Shirley Hall

The Fire Will Purify

At the edge of the forest there is revival. That is where the fire begins. It's not hidden. Many will see it. It will grow to a huge blaze. Many will come to extinguish it. Once they get close to the fire, they will bring good to the forest and no longer want to put the fire out. They will say there is much dead wood in the forest. There is too much rubble and it truly needs to be burned. Many will come to speculate of what is going on. They stand and just watch and have not much emotion. It will not affect them one way or another. They will be complacent. Others now, will jump into the fire to be purified. Those that stand and see a purpose will also jump in and be purified. So, many will come and be purified through this fire. This fire will be a sign to many. It will be a sign of purity. Many will hesitate and say, "Oh, it's too hot!" But the wolves will come behind them and drive them into the fire. (the fear of the enemy will be greater)

After going through the fire, they will arrive on the other side of the forest and will see green. They will see a beautiful sight. They will see a lot of activity. They will see new growth. They will hear new songs sung by the birds. They will see new sights never seen before. They will say, "I never knew this was here before." Then the others will say, "It's always been here, you just see with new eyes." They will pick up a mirror and say, "I don't see new eyes." And the angel of the Lord will hold their hand and take them to a place that will reveal why they see through new eyes. It's a place that's desired by many. It's a place that reveals the Lamb's Book of Life. Once they see their name in this, they will understand why they see differently. When the angel of the Lord escorts them into the forest, they begin to be busy like the others in the forest.

And now also the ax is laid unto the root of the trees:
therefore, every tree which bringeth not forth good fruit is
hewn down and cast into the fire. (Mat 3:10-2)

The fire in this story represents revival. People will react differently to this revival which is depicted in this story. As people go through revival, they will experience transformation including how they view life. The Holy Spirit is compared to fire in the Bible and is the best purifier for man.

Just like a natural fire the Holy Spirit will burn all that can be burned. The Holy Spirit removes all that needs to be removed. What remains is necessary for spiritual growth. I learned that this is very similar to a fire in the forest.

The Chameleon

See that lizard? He moves quickly. He's sleek. Many can change colors according to their backgrounds. When their background is fresh and full of life, they can look this way (I saw a green lizard). When their background is lifeless and so full of dryness, they can look this way. (I saw a brown lizard) So a lizard can appear many ways.

Just like my people, they too look like their surroundings. Just like the lizard, they look like this as a defense. But I say it's not a defense, in man's case, because it is very offensive.

> *And do not be conformed to this world, but be transformed by*
> *the renewing of your mind, that you may prove what is that*
> *good and acceptable and perfect will of God. (Rom. 12:2)*

It's by My Spirit

There were these fleas. They were jumping on a trampoline. They did not even create a bounce in the trampoline. For what movement they created was of their own. (Their bouncing up and down) They spent many hours doing this only to realize that their efforts were futile in trying to get the trampoline to move.

I say, this is so like My people. They put tremendous effort into the movement of My Spirit. But I say that this is not of me. I have not said, move. They move on their own accord. They go without Me. Now for all those fleas, they still go back and try to get that trampoline to move. But I say, until I send you, don't go.

What a perfect illustration of man trying to do something without God. I remember this lesson as I seek God for guidance in my life. I surely do not want to waste time like the fleas. I truly do not want to go and do anything without God. All of us find ourselves, at times, trying to move God, but hopefully we recognize it is futile.

I am the vine, you are the branches. He who abides in Me, and I in him,
bears much fruit; for without Me you can do nothing. (John 15:5)

Use All God Has Given

Vision- I saw a ladybug crawling- (male and females are both called ladybug)

I saw a ladybug crawl up a huge wall. He began to climb and climb. He said, "God would never have me climb up this wall, it is too hard and is too long of a journey." So, the ladybug climbed back down off the wall. Then he ran right into God. God said to the ladybug, "I told you to go up that wall." The ladybug shook his head (in total disbelief) and said to himself, "God would not ask me to climb that wall because it is too hard and too long of a journey." He then walked away and then spread his wings and flew away.

The Lord said, "If my people would use <u>all</u> that I have given them, the journey would not be as long and as hard."

This was an amusing illustration but is a realistic way people respond to God. People walk in unbelief because they will not believe what God's Word says. As this ladybug argued with God it reminded me how we can be. What a simple truth for the body of Christ and it was told in such a palatable way. He wants us to walk in all that He has given us. He equipped us by sending the Holy Spirit so that we are able to accomplish all that God calls us to accomplish.

The Lord helped me to understand how important it is to lean upon His understanding instead of my own. Like the ladybug, it had the wings, the ability to get up the wall. Yet, it flew away in defeat. How ironic! The Lord emphasized to use what He gave me. The Holy Spirit gives us all the power we need. All we need to do is exercise our spiritual gifts and use the wisdom the Holy Spirit gives us. We need only to recognize what we have been given and to use everything to its fullest.

Because of this simple story and vision, I gained a passion to pray even more in the Holy Spirit's language. The Holy Spirit is our teacher, comforter and one in which we receive guidance. I try to draw upon the Holy Spirit as much as possible because of the empowerment He provides. I feel saddened that people are depending less on the Holy Spirit and more on human ability. The Word is for us to use and as we pray the Word, it gives us power. As we apply the Word it transforms us. When we use the Word as a plumb line for decision making, we become wise. What great resources by combining the wisdom of the Holy Spirit with the Word! POWERFUL!

The Fire in The Forest

Vision- I saw a forest with many animals dashing around jumping and leaping as they detected a huge fire

Listen to the excitement!
Listen to the people!
He's Coming Soon!
It's like the fire in the forest. The closer it gets the animals run in a heightened excitement. They know their surrounding and know there is a change, a change that is coming. With the animals the fire is an unknown source, but with my people Jesus is not an unknown source. You know of His coming because He forewarns. He bought you for a price. He'll not mislead! As the fire gets closer, also in the hearts of my people I will create an increase of burning. There will be a frenzy of activity from the enemy also. Many will try to put out the fire but will be unable.

This is a fire that cannot be quenched!

You should have seen those animals running around. What an illustration of intense excitement in the kingdom. I think there is that excitement today for His soon return. God's people, being spiritual beings, sense activity in the spiritual realm. As the men on the road to Emmaus had burning within their hearts as they encountered Jesus so shall we. Be ready for His return!

*And they said to one another, "Did not our heart burn
within us while He talked with us on the road, and while
He opened the Scriptures to us?" (Luke 24:32)*

Do Great Big Things

As a little boy was yet little he yelled out, "I want to be big!" His mother said, "You will be big one day but, as you are little you will do little things and then when you are big you will do big things." So, the little boy finally grew and grew until he was fully grown. When he was fully grown his mother said, "Now, you are fully grown and have grown big as your heart has desired." "Now, what big things shall you accomplish?" The young man stared at her and questioned her statement, "What do you mean?" She repeated herself as she did long ago, "When you are little you will do little things and now that you are big you shall do big things. The young man shook his head and assured her he, now, understood.

Then the Lord said, "I say this too, to my people." "They must begin to do the greater things as they have become great in the kingdom" So, I say, "Do as I do." "Do as I say." "When you do these things, in these ways, you will accomplish GREAT BIG THINGS!"

This is a story of encouragement. We must come to the Lord as a little child to enter God's kingdom, yet we must mature in the ways of the Spirit and move forward into greater things.

*"Most assuredly, I say to you, he who believes in Me, the
works that I do he will do also; and greater works than these
he will do, because I go to My Father. (John 14:12)*

Come Up Higher

Once upon a time, there was this snake. He crawled all through the grass and all through the woods all around him. As he crawled, he only saw the grass in his midst. Even when he'd go to new places, he saw the grass. The grass varied a bit, but not much.

Now, there was a bird. He flew all over, up mountains and up in the tallest trees. This bird flew all around and saw great sights because he was at a great height. Now for the snake, he could not see far because of his position. But the bird had a position that allowed him to see at a greater distance and at a greater perspective.

So, which is best? To see what the snake saw or what the bird saw? I say, for My people, I want them to come up higher to see better, to see from a different perspective. I want them to see as I see, for I see much greater. For My kingdom is on a much greater height, depth, and width. It is for My people to know, and be, and be conformed to my likeness.

This day is yours to know of My kingdom!

Feeding Flesh

Vision- I saw a huge fat seal flapping its flippers

I saw a seal. I saw that it did a task and then I saw someone throw it a fish for doing the task.

The Lord said, "Don't always expect something for each task." "It only feeds the flesh."

A Fish Out of Water

There once was a fish. He would swim but delighted in seeing the birds above. He would gaze at them and delight in their flight. He longed to know what it was like to fly. He pondered on ways that he too could fly. He thought, "Now if I could swim so fast, I could go from the water and enter the air." But then he thought long and hard. He thought that maybe there would be danger entering the air in this manner. So, he thought again. Once more he came up with a good idea. He said, "Now if I could just flip myself up out of the water, maybe God would give me wings and then I would fly." Again, he thought and figured this was not the will of God.

Then the Lord said… For I say, stay where you are, doing what I have created you to do. Do not come up with ways to maneuver yourself into things not designed for you. For I have a plan for each of you. My plan is perfect. My plan is a plan of all plans. I shall tell you of things you should enter. Do not be like a fish out of water for you shall surely die.

Whenever I desire to do what other people are doing, I am reminded of this story. Each of us has been created for a particular purpose in God's kingdom. Each gifting in us is unique to the fulfillment of those purposes. It never works well when we try to be like someone else. Realizing what you are created for brings great joy and fills you with such completeness. As we seek God for our purpose, He will be faithful to reveal it.

For in Him dwells all the fullness of the Godhead bodily; and you are complete in Him, who is the head of all principality and power. (Col 2:9-10)

CHAPTER 10

Evidence That God Inhabits Our Praise

"But thou art holy, O thou that inhabits the praises of Israel." (Ps.22:3 KJV)

I have always been very interested in the scripture where it encourages us to worship God in Spirit and in truth. Somehow, I always think it means more than what we comprehend. Each one of us might have a different understanding according to our own experiences. It could mean a time where we are completely consumed with Him and completely surrendered to Him during worship. I have experienced many times the presence of the Lord during worship and have also felt deeply moved during those times.

But the hour is coming, and now is, when the true worshipers will worship the Father in spirit and truth; for the Father is seeking such to worship Him. (John 4:23)

I presume that worshipping God in spirit and truth describes God as being on the receiving end, yet we get to enjoy the benefits of it. I think I might have experienced a taste of worshipping Him in Spirit and truth at a conference, many years ago, in Lakeland Florida.

I was in a church, that held ten thousand people, and it was packed. During this week of the conference I heard countless testimonies of miraculous happenings from people who had traveled from around the

United States and beyond. People were sharing non-stop about their encounters with God during that conference. You could look at their faces and recognize how moved people were. My friend and I had never encountered anything so miraculous. God's presence was powerful! Just making a trip to the restroom was an adventure of remarkable testimonies about what God was doing in the lives of these people. People were hearing His voice, having visions and were experiencing healings physically and emotionally. It was incredible and extremely exciting the entire week.

One of the nights, during worship, something very unique began to happen. Everyone seemed to be so focused on the Lord. The worship continued for quite some time when people began to worship by the Holy Spirit. Thousands of people everywhere began singing in their heavenly, God given, language. As everyone sang in tongues there began to be a unity in the Holy Spirit I had never experienced before. It was a corporate unity and it was powerful. I too, had joined in the singing in tongues, but I began to notice a pause, then a release by the Holy Spirit for my individual part. It was like God assigned each of us our very own part to sing. Thousands of people were flowing together in unison in a new song of the Lord.

It was the most beautiful sound I had ever heard!

Every few seconds I felt the Holy Spirit rise up inside of me, for my part, and I would sing it. I sang just a little piece of this finely orchestrated song of the Lord. This corporate worship seemed to be the closest to worshipping Him in Spirit and in truth that I have ever experienced. It lasted for such a long time. At the climax of this beautiful orchestration of God a band of angels could be heard. I could hear a level that seemed to be above us, in a physical sense, where you could hear melodious, gentle singing. It's hard to explain a spiritual experience in physical terms. When it ended there was such a holy hush, a sweet presence of our Lord. It was like liquid love all around. This experience has shown me a definite evidence that God exists, and He inhabits our praise. He enters into our praise and worship as we allow ourselves to completely surrender to Him.

I often ponder on that experience with God and His body of believers and I so long for that again. I occasionally feel frustrated during worship. I think we fall short right at the point when we are on the brink of something miraculous during worship. We stop short of an incredible experience with God. If we could just wait upon Him…. If we could just linger a little longer…. If we could just press into Him a little harder! I realize that there is so much more we are missing because of our hurriedness. Many are worshipping through flesh instead of with a sincere heart of worship. He ripped the veil in the temple giving us full access to Him and His presence, yet, we are in too big of a hurry during worship. It is all about lavishing our love upon Him and being in His presence!

That is where it ALL happens!

I was worshipping in my living room one afternoon and I was caught up in the Lord. I began to see myself in a vision. As I was worshipping God and loving Him with all my heart, I saw myself quickly and easily enter a tent like structure. I knew it was the Holy of Holies. I looked up and saw Jesus standing at a chalkboard. He was writing something on the board when, suddenly, He pulled the writing off the chalkboard like a strip and sent it to me. As it wrapped around the top of my head He said, "I will give you the mind of Christ!" Again, He wrote on the chalkboard, but this time when He pulled it off, He shot it into my heart! He spoke, "And I will engrave My words upon your heart!" The next thing I knew, Jesus was standing by my side and He took my hand and took me out of the Holy of Holies and took me to the edge of a steep hill. He pointed out over a city and began to tell me that He would take me to people. Instantly, we were off the hill down in the city. Jesus and I were standing before a man that was sitting down on a sidewalk gambling. I began to stoop down to the man when the Lord stopped me. The Lord leaned down and stood the man upright before me. Jesus said to me, "You do not have to go down to their level because I am going to bring them up to you."

> For "who has known the mind of the Lord that he may instruct Him?" But we have the mind of Christ. (1 Cor 2:16)

I had several revelations from this vision. Number one, I realized that through worship we are able to easily enter into His presence and encounter

Him. During these close encounters with Him, the Lord can impart His word to us. He can teach us and give us revelations concerning His word. He was giving me specific directions in how He would use me regarding people. I was not supposed to go to places and stoop to their level, but that He was going to bring them to me. I encourage you to focus intently on the Lord during worship. Once we enter into a special place with Him, we are able to see and hear Him with clarity. He wants to show us so much and wants to teach us His ways.

> *For this is the covenant that I will make with the house of Israel after those days, says the Lord: I will put My laws in their mind and write them on their hearts; and I will be their God, and they shall be My people. (Heb 8:10)*

One time, during worship at church I desperately wanted to encounter the Lord. I wanted to feel His presence! As my eyes were closed, I found myself so desirous for God. I wanted to see Him! I wanted to hear from Him. Oddly, I began to use my spiritual eyes and look for Him. I began to have a vision. I saw all these boxes in front of me obstructing my view. I walked up to them and I aggressively knocked them out of my way to clear the way so I could see the Lord. I knew He was there, and nothing could keep me from Him! Then, as I looked up, I saw Him up in front of me to the right. I ran toward Him with expediency and stopped abruptly when I tired. I saw Him reach down into a river with His hand and He threw it at my belly. When it hit my belly, a river formed from me. As I looked up again Jesus was far off to the left of me. Again, I ran toward Him with expediency and stopped abruptly when I tired. Again, He leaned down into a river with His hand and threw a ball of water and it hit my stomach. Again, a river formed. This also happened for a third time. Jesus had His eye on me throughout this whole event. Each time I stopped to get my breath he would turn His head slightly to see if I was coming. He always waits for us!

> *In the last day, that great day of the feast, Jesus stood and cried, saying, If any man thirst, let him come unto me, and drink. He that believeth on me, as the scripture hath said, out of his belly shall flow*

rivers of living water. (But this spake he of the Spirit, which they that
believe on him should receive: for the Holy Ghost was not yet given;
because that Jesus was not yet glorified.) (John 7:37-38KJV)

As we seek God, we will find Him. He wants us to find Him! Worship is that special time where the Lord meets us. He inhabits the praises of His people. That is His way! He promises to meet us there, right in the midst of praise and worship. Take this opportunity to meet Him there too. He will show Himself to us in many different ways, but He surely will be faithful to be there in the midst of that complete surrender of our worship of Him. At that particular time, I felt so desperate for Him. His word says when we thirst for Him to go to Him. As we believe in Him, we will be amazed at what will flow out of us. As the Holy Spirit is within us, He can freely flow out to minister. The vision perfectly lined up with scripture unbeknown to me at the time. I did not have much comprehension about the endless possibilities of the Great God that I served!

One afternoon, I was praising and worshipping the Lord in my living room. I turned on the CD player and popped in one of my favorite cds and was having a great time praising the Lord. I was having an awesome time! I was singing and twirling around and just felt an overwhelming amount of love for the Lord and from the Lord. Spontaneously, right in the middle of my exuberant praise and worship I yelled out, "Lord, I didn't even think you liked women!" (Where did that deep thought come from?) Instantaneously and undoubtedly, I heard, "I first appeared to a woman before I went to my Father!" My response was, "You did?" I then ran to the Bible and looked up the story. There it was! (John 20:16-18) I was quite shocked to hear such a quick response from the Lord. He always seems to amaze me while simultaneously surprising me! For me, the evidence is overwhelming that He inhabits the praise of His people. And…He truly does love women.

At times, I have felt irritated when people complain about a particular style of worship or that it's too loud or it's not this or that. I look at praise and worship as something between the Lord and me and I am responsible to connect with Him. It is nice if the worship is conducive to enter into His presence, but it is all up to us to draw near to Him and saturate ourselves with Him instead of our surroundings.

As we draw near to Him He will draw near to us!

Over the years I found a type of worship that I dearly loved. I discovered someone that really knew how to worship God and knew how to bring many others along with him. His name was Kim Clement. He has since gone to be with the Lord, but I have never encountered any praise and worship such as this. For one, the worship was usually three hours long. Often, it takes a little bit of time to get our thoughts off ourselves and for our focus to solely be directed toward the Lord. This worship not only allowed for time to change focus from man-centered to God-centered, but it ushered in God's presence as people completely surrendered to Him.

Kim Clement and His worship team began to praise God with some special known songs then abandoned them shortly thereafter. From then on, it was spontaneous praise straight from the heart. It was very close to being completely Holy Spirit led. Once high praises ended, after about an hour and a half, then came intense, sincere, heartfelt worship. It seemed to always end with a beautiful stillness and awe-inspiring presence of the Lord. Deep breath….just remembering how it felt! Now that I have explained what happened externally, let me try to explain what happened deep inside.

At first, it was very exciting just like most worship experiences. Eventually I would find myself getting lost in the Lord. I would find that the people around me disappeared. They were there, but they did not have much effect on what I was experiencing. The corporate worship was amazing, but it was as if I had the complete attention of the Lord and He certainly had my complete attention. The more I went into His presence and felt Him all around me, the more connected I felt. It was like I would come up to a level and then in fifteen more minutes I was exceeding that level. I just kept going up higher and higher and higher. It was a feeling of being ecstatic like I have never felt before. I was experiencing all the feelings of love, joy, freedom, peace and excitement all rolled into one. Whew! And on top of that, Kim also had a prophetic anointing and somehow that began to be imparted to me during the worship. I could hear the Lord speaking to me so clearly. Jesus would show me things through visions during worship. Inwardly, I had a heart of sincere worship that continued all through the night where I felt extremely close to God. Even when I went back to the hotel and finally went to sleep, it was like I was awake all-night having visions and I continued worshipping in my sleep. It was incredible for me all the while drawing me closer and closer in intimacy with my Savior! Most times I would jot down notes, so I would not forget anything. It was simply awesome, and the Lord was endlessly breathtaking. That could be what it means to worship Him in spirit and truth.

I traveled many times to Detroit to experience that worship and took my husband and children. That was around twenty years ago, and my kids still sing those spontaneous praise songs. It was powerfully transforming and truly evident that God inhabits our praise and worship!

Worship brings us near to God as He inhabits that worship. I have experienced sheer joy during worship whether through laughter or through tears. Worship is a time we give it all to Him! It's a time we meet with Him. Many times, healing occurs as we worship. As He inhabits our true and sincere worship, He is able to work many miracles in our lives.

All people go through tragedy at some point in their life. Our family had something very tragic happen eight years ago. Our youngest daughter had come to spend the night along with her six-week-old baby, Lucas. Early that next morning, I found that he had died in his sleep in his bed. I tried to resuscitate him, but he was gone. The whole family cried and wept uncontrollably. It was a nightmare. I remember crying out to Jesus over and over. Words cannot express the horror we experienced that day and the coming days. It was so horrifying to us and the grief was smothering. Our family had never encountered such darkness as with the grief over this sweet baby's sudden death. Each family member was dealing with the intensity of the grief in different ways. For several days, my husband and I were barely able to breathe. It was so heavy, and we had never experienced such a sudden and dreadful tragedy. I just remember my husband and I sitting on the couch, listless and taking deep breaths. It was something neither of us fathomed and the weight of what had just occurred seemed to be crushing us. I also had this deep dark fear come up on me. I put night lights in my room, and I kept the temperature in the house ten degrees warmer than I normally did. I think I was going through some sort of shock and it lasted several months. I had never had such terror come on me and I could see my husband was experiencing the same thing.

On the second day of this crushing grief, my husband and I were on the couch. We could not eat, speak, and could barely breathe. I had never experienced grief to that degree. I believe God gave me an answer to help comfort us and to lift the heaviness. I thought of putting on a worship cd. We listened to it over and over for around two hours and cried and praised God. We still had enormous grief, but the crushing inability to get our breath lifted. We were able to breath normally again. There was relief through that worship because **He** was in it. He came to comfort us in our greatest hour of need.

I know God is with us in exceptional times and through devastating times. He, by His Holy Spirit, will comfort us during those days we just don't think we will make it. The death of our baby made the whole family closer. We clung to one another once we realized how short life could be. I thank the Lord for being there getting us all through it and that He honored His word that says He will never leave us nor forsake us.

To console those who mourn in Zion, to give them beauty for ashes, the oil of joy for mourning, the garment of praise for the spirit of heaviness; That they may be called trees of righteousness, the planting of the Lord, that He may be glorified. (Is. 61:3)

CHAPTER 11

Evidence that God Directs

A man's heart plans his way, But the Lord directs his steps. (Prov 16:9)

God has always given direction to people. Sometimes He was very specific and other times He remained vague. His specifics for constructing the temple were extremely detailed. On the other hand, Abraham was told to sacrifice his only son without knowing why. Either way, God is looking for our obedience. At times the direction does not make sense from a human standpoint. It's truly all about trust! I often wonder what the Israelites thought as they marched around the wall of Jericho in silence. God was clever requiring their silence. I can only imagine the grumblings of unbelief they may have uttered. Then, trumpets sound and all let out a shout and down came the walls! Obedience produces results! (Josh 6:20)

Once Jesus came, He too, gave many directions to people before and after the resurrection. Now that Jesus has ascended to and is seated at the right hand of the Father, the Holy Spirit has been sent to lead us and give us direction. While Jesus was on earth, He too was led By the Holy Spirit. As the Holy Spirit directed Paul and Timothy they were forbidden to preach in parts of Asia. It is essential to be led by the Holy Spirit today. As we receive direction from God it is equally as important to be obedient to that directive.

For as many as are led by the Spirit of God, these are sons of God. (Ro 8:14)

As I was praying one day, I heard the Lord tell me to go to the mall and pray for people. I had no idea what and how that would be accomplished, but I began to pray to get further wisdom on my first directive. As I was praying, I saw a vision of balloons, just balloons. I had no idea what that meant, but I was going forward in faith. I knew I was to go to the local mall and pray for people and I saw balloons. That was all that the Lord revealed to me to go forward in obedience. I was excited to see what would come next in this new adventure that God was calling me to do.

I got up early on Saturday morning and headed for the local mall. I knew I was to arrive before the mall opened. I had been praying all morning and was encouraged by the Lord. I felt empowered by the Holy Spirit and could not have felt readier to be obedient to God. I continued to pray as I drove to the mall. A train stopped me at a railway track, and I had been sitting for a moment when, suddenly, I hear words, "Go up to the guy in the truck in front of you and tell him I love him." Really? Those words were not lining up with going to the mall and so I sat and sat and was scared to jump out of my vehicle. Here I was on a mission from God and could not even do what God was asking me to do in that moment. You know how it is! One moment you are filled with boldness of a lion and then, the next minute, you are as weak as a little mouse that can barely squeak! If I had only known what was ahead of me for that day, I surely would have done something as simple as just telling someone that Jesus loved them. Well, the train went by and I missed the opportunity to be obedient in my small task! I felt mad at myself for not being quick to be obedient.

Even though I was frustrated at myself for already failing that little test I continued my mission with gusto. I continued to drive to the mall, asked for forgiveness, and got myself back to focusing on the task at hand. When I got close to the mall I began to listen intently to the Lord's leading. I asked the Lord which parking area to go to. I was impressed to turn in to a particular area and so the next question I asked the Lord was which door to go into? I saw a door and heard Him speak, "There!" I turned in and parked, all the while praying and talking to God.

I entered the mall and walked by Toys-R-Us and down the hall into the corridor of the mall. I continue thinking of the balloons I had seen in the vision. In just a few moments I come up on a showcase. There! There was a whole showcase full of balloons. That was the spot! I looked around and saw a bench. I was very much impressed and excitedly eager. I was thinking how God made this so easy. I sat down on the bench and waited to see what God was going to do next. I looked around and unexpectantly I noticed something very peculiar. People were walking all around the edges of the hallway for exercise. At that time, I did not know people did that. So, I sat and prayed for people as they went around and around the parameter of the mall. The Lord would give me specific things to pray for each person that passed by my little bench with the showcase of beautiful balloons. I prayed for people's marriages, their jobs, family relationships and whatever God put on my heart to pray. This was great! I was doing just what I did every day of my life, praying and interceding for others.

I spent many early morning Saturdays sitting on my bench praying for the walkers, long after my balloons were taken out of the showcase. I never forgot how faithful God was in directing me every step of the way to do such a simple thing. I never forgot how I was disobedient to get out of my car to tell someone of His love for them. I always hope to never fail in my response to my Lord, but I know I do, and I will. Those lessons are well learned and hopefully they become fewer and fewer. I earnestly want to please the Lord, hear His voice, and then be obedient when He directs.

For He is our God, and we are the people of His pasture,
And the sheep of His hand. Today, if you will hear His
voice: "Do not harden your hearts (Ps.95:7-8a)

Another time many years ago, while I was journaling the Lord was showing me a place, He was going to take me. I saw a vision of South America and I drew a picture of it in my journal. A few weeks later I was at a Christian Aglow International meeting. At the end of the night the speaker began praying for people. When he got to me, he began praying, then he prophesied, "You're going someplace to minister in South America." I shook my head yes and felt excited for the confirmation. Then he said, "Lord, where in South America?" The man then said, "Chili". "God is going to take you to Chili." I am still waiting for that prophetic word to come to pass. I know it was specific direction for a place I am supposed to go someday. The opportunity has never opened for that yet, but I still look for it and wait for it. I am getting a little older and wonder when that will happen. I feel like I will be part of a ministry team at some point for that ministry trip.

Because I feel fairly confident that I hear from the Lord I understand quite well what I am supposed to engage in and what activities I do not need to be doing. It is a good feeling to have that kind of direction in my life. I think it has saved me time and energy on things I have not been called to do. You too, can experience divine direction as you seek God's will.

I remember many years ago my mother had a feeling she might have cancer. She began to pray, and the Lord spoke to her to call her doctor. The Lord told her that her doctor would be on vacation, but she was to go ahead and make an appointment to get checked. When she called the doctor's office the secretary told her that the doctor was on vacation just as the Lord had told her. In a normal situation my mother would have put off the appointment, but because the Lord told her specific details she followed His direction.

When the doctor returned, she went to her appointment. He had her follow up with a DNC. Sure enough, she had uterine cancer. She immediately had a hysterectomy and the cancer was removed. That is evidence that God gives us direction. As she heard the God's voice and was obedient, it prolonged her life for many years.

Direction came in a dream to pray a few years ago for a friend's daughter. My friend's daughter went to prison regarding a car accident. It was tragic for all involved. I normally do not feel that God allows us to experience fear for His purpose. Although, I realized that He would if He was trying to warn us of something. For the first time, in a dream, I experienced extreme fear for the sole reason… to pray.

In my dream I was in prison. I was lying in bed in prison and I was petrified. I was so terrified that I was shaking. Then, I woke up! Immediately, while still trembling, I thought about my friend's daughter and knew I was to pray for her for intense fear while she was in prison. Seriously, I prayed for two hours for that girl. I did not even know the girl, yet, God allowed me to feel what she was feeling. I was shaken with fear which gave me great empathy for this young girl. I kept thinking that I should call my friend and tell her what happened, but I let time pass and I never called. Several weeks later another friend called and shared with me about our mutual friend's daughter experiencing intense nightmares while in prison. I then knew the reason for my dream. God is so precious that He cared that much for that young girl. Amazingly, He cares that much about each one of us. Later, I was able to share with her mother about praying for her daughter, but God would have gotten great glory if I had been obedient and called her at the time. I had never experienced anything like that nor have I since.

There are many times when God gave me direction but, somehow, the stories ended up in other chapters. As I am thinking about God's direction, I am reminded of the countless times He has spoken to pray for someone, call someone or help someone. We often question whether it was a directive from God. The more we go forward toward the promptings of our heart I think we will find the answer to that question. Sometimes the Holy Spirit will direct us to just speak up while never knowing what impact it might have upon others. Be brave, be bold, and have faith! Lean in and hear His voice!

HE TRULY IS REMARKABLE!

The steps of a good man are ordered by the Lord, And He delights in his way. Though he fall, he shall not be utterly cast down; For the Lord upholds him with His hand. I have been young, and now am old; Yet I have not seen the righteous forsaken, Nor his descendants begging bread.
(Ps 37:23-25)

CHAPTER 12

Evidence Of God's Creativity

For we are His workmanship, created in Christ Jesus for good works, which God prepared beforehand that we should walk in them. (Eph 2:10)

It is no surprise to characterize God as being creative. All you have to do is look around. Nothing is replicated in cookie cutter fashion. All animals are unique in appearance and unique in the way they live. Look at mankind itself. Each person has distinguishable fingerprints, and none are alike. While watching a documentary once, they explained that even each person's ears are unique. As we look at nature, we see such beauty and such a variety. All the way down to the microscopic world we see such creativity. In the next story I saw how God used me to be creative. He was being creative through me.

I realize that I have said this before, but God has surprised me so many times. He's literally caught me off guard in the most unique and unusual ways. It is His personality to be surprising. I imagine how lively He probably was with His friends. I assure you; He astounded each one of the disciples. Can you imagine the surprise when Jesus called Peter to come to Him as He was walking on water toward the boat? He told Peter to step out of a boat, onto water, and walk. I imagine the disciples were very shocked as they witnessed Peter as he stepped out of the boat. Peter trusted Jesus to take that first step. In my years of walking with the Lord I have learned to trust Jesus because of all that I have seen Him do. I'm still learning to trust Him with unwavering faith. I assume that will take me until I breathe my last breath here on earth.

This story tells of one of the greatest surprises that the Lord has ever sprung on me! It was a sudden, unsuspecting call on my life. I thought He could not surprise me as much as He had already, but I was wrong! When He first started speaking to me, He said I was going to have an exciting life. I could not have asked for more excitement! Over these many years my walk with Jesus has truly been astonishing and beyond exciting. Every time He speaks to me it is thrilling. Watching Him work in the lives of others is sensational. With every vision and every story, He tells, comes intrigue. He keeps me watching and listening and waiting for His next move. It truly is a great way to live, to live with continual expectation.

I was soon approaching my summer break from teaching for the year and was pondering what I would do for the summer. My daughter was in high school and one afternoon I nonchalantly asked her if she would think it would be fun to write a children's book together. She always liked school and she responded quickly with a yes. I had never done anything like that, but for some reason, I had this thought about trying to write a book.

The first week school was out I had professional development classes. I had taken a class that was about children's literature. The speaker, as a classroom teacher, was telling us how he discovered a way to get children interested in reading. He told us how every time he read a book to the class it really drew their interest for that particular book.

Usually, during these professional development courses there are many of my colleagues and we sit in a group. However, this time was different. There were no other teachers from my school attending that session even though it was held in a very large auditorium. I sat alone and began to talk to the Lord. As I contemplated about the book my daughter and I would write I wondered what type of book it would be. I stopped and prayed silently, "Lord, do you want me to write a book that is academic or a book from the heart?" I heard loud and clear, "A book from the heart!" So as soon as I heard this, I began drawing a heart on my stenographers note pad. I also wrote the words a book from the heart on the notepad.

Suddenly, the man teaching the literature session held up a book and began to describe it, "Now this is a book of the heart!" It immediately got my full attention. Then again, he said, "This is a real book of the heart!"

And for the third time he repeats how this book that he loved was a real book of the heart. I about fell out of my seat.

This changes everything!

Not only was this something I had thought I would do, it now was something God was calling me to do. He had just put His fingerprint on it with a specific direction. I knew that voice and recognized His leading by getting that specific confirmation. I immediately got enormously enthusiastic. I was downright giddy! When I got home, I shared my experience with my husband. For a couple of days, I tossed around how I would begin. On the second day after the conference session I was up late at night and alone. I pulled out the computer and opened power point. I opened several pages and started to find clipart and started to pop a funny character and some background onto pages. Then, I just started to type. In a matter of an hour I had written my first children's book called "The Poppets". I did not think on it or plan what I was going to write. It just flowed out. It had to be the Holy Spirit because it just came up and out.

The next couple of weeks I wrote 7 children's books. Each time I gathered some clipart on a particular character, or characters, and added some simple background in power point and just began to type. Again, I did not plan on what to write. I seriously take no credit other than being obedient. It was the evidence of a creative God pouring through me. I wonder, sometimes, if He just wanted to write some children's books and I was willing. Being a first-grade teacher, I naturally loved children's books. That's what seemed so special to me because He was doing something that He knew I loved! He did that to bless me!

What was amazing to me was that these stories had complex patterns. A couple books had repetitive text. One of the books, "A Fairy Tale", was a parable. After the first three sentences I said out loud, "This is a parable!" It also had patterns that I can assure you I did not design. It just flowed out. "A Fairy Tale" was a story about a fairy that struggled with knowing her purpose. Eventually, she discovered what she was created for which parallels our own Christian walk. My family expressed that they really liked the books as well. They all encouraged me by telling me that I might have something with these stories. I know I keep saying this, but the Lord always amazes me!!! Even my husband thought they were really good, and he is not easily impressed. I could not and did not take the credit, I made sure I gave credit to God because the words just flowed out. It just now came to me…the children's books really did come from the heart as the Lord said. He placed the words in my heart…and out of the abundance of the heart the mouth speaks. I have new meaning of that scripture! As we are filled with God's Spirit great abundance is able to flow from each of us.

I taught first grade when I wrote all the books and my students loved them. They helped me decide which book to publish first. They chose a book called "Buggy Buggy". I realized it was a hit when my students were chanting the repetitive part of the text while on a field trip. I also let my students pick the covers and vote on the ones they liked the best. I had the perfect audience because the books are for elementary age children. Several schools have invited me in for career day in order to read my books and tell the students about being an author.

I eventually had several books illustrated by local artists and had three of them published. I am publishing the book "Sorenson" along with this book. I still have several I would love to get published but have not to date. Knowing my God, He will bless what He gives, so, I wait patiently!

Occasionally, I think I ought to sit down and see what happens. The Lord gave me 7 children's books and then I wrote a book about manners called "Norman Knows". I wrote it to teach my students proper manners while in public places. I also wrote "Fluffy Cat" which was about our pet cat and gave each of my kids a book for Christmas. Everyone seems to have their favorite book. Each one is completely different except for the trilogy with repetitive text that stems from the book "Buggy Buggy".

My desire is that someday I will write more children's books because I really love them. They are so fun to read, and I love the innocence in them. Unlike most people, I have **never** had any ambitions to write books. It has always been something the Lord has asked me to do and I in turn acted in obedience. I recall, many years, ago when the Lord told me that I would write many books. At that time, I had only written one book and it didn't seem possible. As of now I have written 11 books called of the Lord. I am getting up in years, and I know I will accomplish exactly what the Lord calls me to do. Who knows what kinds of creativity He will pour through me in the future?

Thanks Jesus! You're Fun!

CHAPTER 13

Evidence That God Gives Visions

Now there was a certain disciple at Damascus named Ananias; and to him the Lord said in a vision, "Ananias." And he said, "Here I am, Lord." So, the Lord said to him, "Arise and go to the street called Straight, and inquire at the house of Judas for one called Saul of Tarsus, for behold, he is praying. And in a vision, he has seen a man named Ananias coming in and putting his hand on him, so that he might receive his sight." (Acts 9:10-12)

There is strong evidence in the old and new testaments of the Bible that God uses visions to communicate. The word vision or visions is used over one hundred times in the Bible. Even when the word is not used, specifically, there are many times where there is a description of seeing a vision. Jesus Himself states that He does nothing unless He sees His Father doing it. I believe He is seeing what His Father is doing in vision form.

Jesus gave them this answer: "Very truly I tell you, the Son can do nothing by himself; he can do only what he sees his Father doing, because whatever the Father does the Son also does. For the Father loves the Son and shows him all he does. (John 5:9-10)

From the time that I began to hear the Lord with greater clarity, I began to have these continual pictures as He spoke to me. They occurred the entire time the Lord was teaching me to hear His voice. As I listened to Him, I had many visualizations. At first, I did not know to call them visions. They were very natural as they occurred and eventually, I realized what they were. As the Lord gave me these images, He would explain how they were related to what He was teaching. He used the pictures as examples, and they had spiritual significance to what He was explaining to me. I grew so accustomed to these visions that they became commonplace and they continued to occur as I prayed.

For me, these visions are just quick glimpses of an image and then I usually have a revelation about them. During prayer I have many images and they usually come before the revelation. It is like a picture show and it really helps me to pray according to what the Holy Spirit shows me. Some of these quick glimpses are humorous and they seem unrelated to what I am praying. Then the Lord shows a particular aspect to pray according to that vision. It then makes complete sense.

Just today at prayer group I saw an olive with the pimiento inside. The Holy Spirit had me pray concerning where man has inserted things into what God had created. Of course, that pimento did not, naturally, belong in the olive. A pit was removed, then someone placed the pimento into the olive. It was a perfect example of representation for that prayer. That sounds funny but that was the vision and the revelatory prayer that went with it. He makes me laugh at some of the similitudes. Similitudes are comparisons between two things or a state or quality of being similar to something. I truly love to pray because it is very interesting to hear and see what God shows me and tells me to pray. Prayer is never boring, as some might convey. If you're praying according to what the Holy Spirit shows, it becomes tremendously fascinating.

It's very exciting!

During Jesus' ministry He came upon Nathanael. He told Nathanael that He saw him sitting by the fig tree (John 1:48). He did not see him physically; He saw him in a vision. Jesus had a vision of Nathanael which in turn caused Nathanael to become a believer. It is a miraculous occurrence. The Old Testament claims that we will have visions (Joel 2:28) The Bible says God will pour dreams and visions out upon people. It repeats that scripture in the New Testament also. This means it is reiterated, repeated, or echoed. Anything that is stated that we can have in scripture means it belongs to the believer. Pray to experience visions. They are very powerful, and they are evidence of God.

> *And it shall come to pass in the last days, saith God, I will*
> *pour out of my Spirit upon all flesh: and your sons and your*
> *daughters shall <u>prophesy</u>, and your young men shall see <u>visions,</u>*
> *and your old men shall <u>dream dreams:</u> (Acts 2:17KJV)*

The Lord wants to bring us into His world which is in a superior realm. We want to join Him in all that is available to us to be able to turn this world upside down for Christ. There is nothing like presenting God as He truly is, using His gifts that He gave. The power resides in God's way and not in our way! A vision that Peter had turned the entire course of salvation to include the gentiles. As God gave Peter this powerful vision, he then in turn began preaching the gospel to non-Jewish people. Peter saw that the Holy Spirit was given to them too, therefore, made him realize the gospel was for all people. The vision along with the evidence of people being baptized in the Holy Spirit confirmed the revelation to Peter. What an impact it made on Peter and the Church as we know it today.

> *He fell into a trance and saw heaven opened and an object like a*
> *great sheet bound at the four corners, descending to him and let*
> *down to the earth. In it were all kinds of four-footed animals of*
> *the earth, wild beasts, creeping things, and birds of the air. And a*
> *voice came to him, "Rise, Peter; kill and eat." (Acts 10:10b-13)*

Of course, my revelations are simple compared to Peter's, yet, I know that our God is not partial to one over another and He will use whoever He desires to impart truth. It is our acknowledgement and our response to what He shows us that is important. As we are obedient to the things God asks of us, we will find it extremely fulfilling. I have found complete fulfillment in my life as God has deposited many jewels in my path. All I have to do is pick them up and use them for His purpose and His glory!

In this chapter I will be telling about visions that I have had. I hope they will inspire you to ask the Lord for visions. Visions help me to pray for

His purpose. When I have a vision, words of guidance and understanding follow. The vision encourages me and builds my faith. The visions I am sharing are given for a variety of reasons. Some were for prayer and others for teaching. Some of these are for revelation. I have had a few visions that served as warnings. Others have been to give direction.

I am going to title some visions and explain what happened or what was taught as a result of the vision. As we see through the eyes of the Holy Spirit our lives can be profoundly changed!

The Baby

I was on my way to work one morning, and I was praying as usual. On this particular morning I had a vision of this baby being left out in the cold. It was a wintery morning and therefore I began to pray fervently about this baby to be found and that someone would get it out of the cold. So, I prayed concerning this along with other things. I never gave it much thought throughout the day. Being an intercessor, I pray a lot of things and don't have the time to ponder a whole lot on everything I pray. But, as soon as I got home from work my husband was sitting in his chair and being the newsworthy man that he is says, "Did you hear about that baby?" I shouted from the other room a bit loud and said, 'What? What happened to the baby?" He then proceeded to tell me about this baby that was left outside and that someone found it that morning. I then shared my story with him.

Some visions I have had were never confirmed like that one, but we must still be faithful and respond to whatever we are privileged to see by the Holy Spirit. I always appreciate when the Lord gives me a confirmation to the things I pray. It greatly encourages me and builds my faith.

The Man in Africa

Once I prayed extensively about an African man that was hiding from three white men. I was completely aware that I was seeing into another country because of the surroundings. I saw specific details such as a solid, beat down dirt ground and wooden buildings. The Holy Spirit gave me specific information concerning this man according to what I saw in the vision. This was a series of visions with specifics from the Lord to pray. My prayer was, undoubtedly, for this man to escape from these men. They were hunting for him and I believe they were going to kill him. I saw him hiding in a water barrel as the three men ran past him. I saw him fleeing in the night and through the woods. I even prayed him into the safety of a couple far off. I could have thought I was imagining it all, but when I heard the precise words of prayer coming out of my mouth, I knew it was not me. Only the Holy Spirit has the perfect prayers of intercession because He is sent from above. I believe someday I will meet my friend and he will tell me all about the night the Lord kept him from harm and gave him the wisdom to find safe harbor.

Sometimes we dismiss things the Lord is showing us because we pass it off as something in our mind or disregard it as being silly. Thankfully, the Lord was determined to get my attention in this next situation.

A Warning

Quite some time ago, I awoke in the middle of the night and had a curiosity about my teenage son. I got up and went downstairs. All the lights were on, but he was not anywhere. He was out of high school and I thought maybe he went to his cousins for a visit and had left the lights on. I went upstairs and sat on the couch and just prayed for a moment. I can't even recall what I was praying about when I saw a vision of my son. It was not a very pleasant glimpse of my son and I pushed it out of my mind. It was so graphic that I just tried to dismiss it. The Lord knew this, so He showed me another picture of something I had been looking for and then I instantly thought that this item might be in my son's room. God is so good! Subsequently, I made another trip to the basement to my son's room.

While getting the item, I heard something coming from the closet that made me investigate. When I opened the door there was my son sitting in a chair wrapped in tons of covers with a space heater turned on. Beside him was a 2-liter bottle filled with water. I was quite shocked to see him, and he was shocked to see me likewise.

Once he came out of the closet he began crying and explaining what was going on. See, two days prior I had suspected my son was smoking pot and I told him I was going to give him a drug test. My suspicion was correct because he was trying to drink as much water as possible and sweat it out in the closet. I told him my story of the vision and coming to his room earlier. He, in turn told me that he envisioned his own death by doing this.

I feel certain that my son probably would have died that night if it had not been for the Lord giving me the two visions. I say this not, solely, because of my visions, but because my son had the same warning. The enemy was trying to wipe him out and throw our family off course, but God had other plans. You know what is scary? It is that both of us ignored the visions. The Lord gave us both a vision of the same thing and we both ignored it. If it had not been for the Lord's love and His persistence with me to go back to my son's room, I have great fear of what we would have found the next day.

Often the Lord gives me visions, more like illustrations, to go with what He teaches me. I love them and find them very humorous at times. Here is one of those.

Too Close

In this vision I saw a frog sitting on the ground and instantly his tongue flew out and consumed a butterfly that was passing by. The Lord said, "See how that frog consumed that butterfly?" "This is how the world consumes one that becomes too close to the world."

As we place ourselves before the Lord instead of before the world, He is faithful to position us exactly where we need to be. If we become too friendly and close with the world, we easily can be snatched up just like this butterfly.

This vision and allegory are visually descriptive to the lesson He is teaching me. He taught me in the very beginning that I would inevitably have to go on this journey with Him, alone.

You May Have to Go Alone

I saw myself in a body of water with a couple of people. It was nighttime and we began to dive down into the water. As we dove deeper, I turned, looked back, and noticed the other two people were not going with me. It caused me to hesitate and I heard the Lord say, "You might have to go alone." I continued to swim deep down into the water. As I swam deeper and deeper, I spied a large rock which was flat on one side. As I got to the rock, I saw flashes of pictures on the face of the rock. At that, the Lord spoke that He wanted to show me many things and that I would have to go it alone. I would not be doing this with other people I would be with Him alone. As I returned to the surface of the water a lifeboat picked me up.

We, as people, want people to go with us when we go places. It is human nature to desire this, but in our walk with God we all have our own individual walk. We are on a journey with Him. My journey will not look like yours and visa-versa. The Lord may show you one thing and then He may show me something else. I have learned to have peace even if others are not having the same experiences that I have. I believe it can be a hindrance to what God wants to do if we wait around for others. It is all between you and Him! It is such a personal relationship with intimacy.

X Marks the Spot

After a conference, I was praying for people and a woman came up and claimed she needed direction for her job. I began to pray for the woman when suddenly, I saw a big X. I prayed, "The X marks the spot!" Then, I continued to pray various things for this woman. Upon finishing she said, "You have no idea what you just prayed!" Then she continued to tell me she was a nurse and that she was wondering if she should change jobs by moving to another hospital. She told me that she worked on the top floor of the hospital and right above her station was where the helicopter lands. She said, "Right above where I work, on the roof, is a giant X for the helicopter to land." She got a great big smile and said, "That answers my question!" I thought that was so cute. God just gave me a vision of a great big X with the words X marks the spot. This was all it took for her to know God was telling her to stay at this job. He is amazing! Those types of encounters show me evidence of a God that knows every detail of our lives. It is evidence that God gives visions.

Here is a humbling word I received in vision form.

Revelation

I was laying over my bed praying when I saw a map of the United States. I saw the hand of God throw gold dust out over the country. It was revelation! I saw people scattered sporadically throughout the United States on the ground with their hands raised. They were receiving the revelation that God was throwing out, but unfortunately, I saw much of the revelation hitting the ground and not being received by man. It was just hitting the ground and disappearing into the earth. I felt saddened that so much of God's revelation was not being received. Then God admonished me. He said, "Even you have not received what you could be receiving!"

I know we all fall short, but this vision encouraged me to press, even more diligently, toward the mark of the high calling in Christ Jesus. I became repentant for sure over this! I felt saddened also. Life in America is so comfortable that I think we do not take our Christian walk very serious. **It's just another thing that We Do!** We must separate ourselves from the ways of the world and enter a new way of living. His ways are so much higher than our ways that we should be looking into, exactly, what that means. I'm trying to get there! I am thankful when God admonishes me. That means He loves me! *For whom the* LORD *loves He chastens. (Heb. 12:6)*

Revelation can reveal who He is and what His Kingdom is about. As we position ourselves before Him and establish that we want to receive from Him, He will meet us. The Word is a huge part of knowing Him, but I found out there was a whole lot more to knowing Him. I love the scripture that states that we live on every word that proceeds out of the mouth of the Lord.

"It is written: 'Man shall not live on bread alone,
but on every word that comes from the mouth of God.'"(Matt 4:4)

I was in church one night during worship and the Holy Spirit took me to the picture show once again. The Spirit began speaking as the vision unfolded. This vision was so realistic!

A Piece of the Rock

Vision- I saw a gigantic hole in the ground resembling where a meteor hit.

There was this great crater in the Earth and many people surrounded it and gazed upon it. They wondered what had caused this great thing. Then, they turned to one another and asked emphatically, "What has caused this?" And suddenly, a man arose out of their midst and said loudly and sternly, "This is THAT which God has thrown to the Earth and has **impacted** the Earth!" Then all the people rejoiced and were very happy. Then all the people ran into the crater and grabbed a piece of ROCK and took it out to the world to share what they had heard.

I can still see this vision. It was so powerful to see all those people run into the crater getting the pieces of rock. What a great illustration of how God's people are to share Jesus (the Rock) with others.

I am very glad that the Lord had me record His words. He instructed me to write from the beginning. It helped me to continue recording throughout all these years. When I prepared to write books, I found countless little pieces of papers where I had jotted visions down and I was able to use many of them to share. I urge you to write down any and all things the Lord gives you. As we record what the Lord shows us it lets Him know we value His words as being significant.

Outpouring

I am still waiting for a vision that my son had to come to pass. He was at a youth camp and while he was worshipping, he had a vision. He came home from camp very excited and told me all about it. In his vision He was sitting at a long wooden table eating with Jesus. Jesus gets up and takes him to the door. As they looked out the door it was pouring rain. Together, they walked out of the door into and through the pouring rain.

As they walked down the street in the pouring rain all the streetlights were lit up on each side of the street. On each side of them were, also, rows of houses and each one was lit up inside.

As soon as he told me the details of this vision, I got very excited. I felt strongly that the Lord gave me revelation of the vision. As soon as he finished telling me about the vision, I told my son that I knew what it meant. I felt that the Lord was saying that He was going to take Phillip through a great outpouring. There would be many people receive Christ by all the homes that were filled with the light. What really popped out at me was this, if God was going to take my son through a great outpouring then, I too, would get to go through it. I know I will experience that Great Outpouring and I await eagerly!

Another vision was the first one where I felt temperature. I could feel the coolness of the hole that I found myself in.

Watch for Holes

One time I was praying in the Spirit and suddenly, I saw myself looking over a hole. I looked into the hole and yelled, "Jesus, are you in there?" Again, I yelled, "Jesus, are you in there?" Instantaneously, I found myself **in** the hole. It was dark and dank, and it did not look like it was going to be so easy to get out. I felt stuck! I looked all around and looked upward.

Then the Lord spoke to me and told me to be careful not to go into things when I didn't know for sure if He was in them. He said that I could find myself in something I could not get out of. Wow! I wouldn't want that to happen! I am glad it was just a realistic vision! I am cautious about getting involved in activities where I'm not called. This vision served as a reminder what this type of involvement could feel like. It was also a reminder concerning any desires to be rebellious to God's will. It was much more detrimental than I wanted to imagine!

The Black Pants

One time I had been looking for a pair of black pants that I could not find for two days. I woke up in the morning and continued to rack my brain where those black pants were. I needed them because I wanted to wear them for spirit day at school and our colors are red and black. Finally, out of desperation, I plopped down on the couch and prayed, "Lord, I really need these pants!" "Will you show me where they are?" Immediately, I had a vision of the black pants. In the vision I saw them on the dryer and saw them slide off the dryer and slide down the side of the dryer against the wall. I instantly jumped up and ran into the laundry room and reached down between the wall and the dryer. I felt my pants where they had slid off of the dryer to the floor and I, excitedly, pulled them out! I got the biggest smile and was so happy. I was high on Jesus that whole day!

These types of experiences prove to me that God hears me and cares about the smallest parts of my life. Those personal encounters, with God, give me tangible evidence that He is real. He is faithful even in the seemingly most insignificant parts of our lives. This, assuredly, caused my faith to soar. I love that God gives His people visions! They allow me to tap into an unseen realm.

The Water Bottle

Several years ago, my prayer team and I were going to a rock concert and pray outside before the concert began. The man that was holding the concert was well known for his graphic and perverted exhibitions during his concerts. Days before going I started seeking the Lord. As I was praying, I saw a vision of me spitting in a bottle of water and taking the bottle to the concert. I immediately thought that I'm not going to do that! I was a little outraged for it seemed very odd to spit in a bottle. I then asked the Lord why I would need to do this.

Instantly, the Lord showed me a vision of Jesus spitting in the mud and placing it upon the blind man's eyes to restore his sight. The Lord revealed to me that as I spit into the bottle of water, I was to take it to the concert and spray the water along the door entrances where the people would cross over into the concert. As they crossed over the threshold into the concert the Lord was going to open their eyes. People would not be able to go to the concert without recognizing the perversion during the concert. They would not be deceived. As soon as the Lord showed me this, I was very eager and was more than willing to be obedient.

A few days later, I took my water and nervously poured it along each door entrance. One of the guards walked up to me and asked if it was holy water. I thought that was funny and told him in uncertain words that it was. I did not even think of it as holy water, but I guess it was. I know this seems silly, but I was shaking because I was so scared to do such a simple thing. God is so patient with us. I understand why Jesus said, "Ye of little faith!"

That was a prophetic act that the Lord had me do. A prophetic act is a physical act done for a spiritual significance. Jesus knew how I felt about the request and knew that I never wanted to do anything that was out of my own ideas. Honestly, at first, this really seemed weird. I did not even know what a prophetic act was, back then. I appreciated that the Lord explained the reasoning and that it was scriptural. He is always willing to meet us where we are and is so willing to help us understand. I never knew of the results of placing the water at each doorway's threshold. I did what I was supposed to do and then left the rest in God's hands to perform His miracle. I am sure many had their eyes opened that night.

As I have gone through the journals I often see where the Lord says, "Do you see?" I think that is so amusing. He knows I am seeing it, but He still asks me. I love Him so much! I am an intercessor and love being with similar people who pray. There is something awesome about being with those that love to pray and have the same heart. There is such a bond. I'm sure pastors like to get together for the same reasons. There are times when likenesses bring us together and other times God uses the differences to get the job done. The five-fold ministry is powerful and is needed desperately in the church today. God uses every part of the body for His purpose. I pray that we encourage one another and value one another for every individual work. There is no work too small. All will earn just rewards in heaven.

For the rest of this chapter I will write a vision and tell what the Lord spoke afterward. All the visions and dreams and stories are copied directly from my journals just as I saw them along with the words I heard. Many are very simplistic, and I realize that He was teaching me to hear His voice just like a little child.

Be Filled

(I saw a balloon flying around with the air coming out which caused the balloon to move)

The balloon is filled, and then can move about on what it was filled with. I want you to move about with that which I have filled you with. (Eph 5:18)

Chew Chew

(I saw the Bible opened and I saw a cow in the middle grazing)

The book is open to you, to feed upon. (like a cow that's grazing) He chews, and chews then regurgitates it and then chews some more. I desire that my people be like the cow. (2Tim2:15)

Draw from me

(I saw several peas in one pod)

There were peas in one pod. They varied in size. The reason they vary in size because one drew more from the plant. This is what I desire my people to do. I desire that they draw more from me. (John 15:4)

Keep Bouncing

(I saw a ball bouncing and slowly stop)

See that ball bouncing? It bounces because someone caused it to bounce. Once bounced, it continues to bounce two or three more times on its own. Once it is still it will not move unless someone comes to bounce it once more. My people are like this. Once I give them strength they go on for a while but, then they lose their bounce. I teach, and I teach and then allow them to soak up all that I have taught. I want it to rejuvenate them into a bounce but, surely, the stillness comes again. (Phil 3:14)

I find myself thinking of this vision often. I pray and ask the Lord to bounce me again at times when I feel I have become lethargic or complacent. We all become complacent at times and we need the Lord to get us moving once again.

Spiritual Blindness and the Circle of Fire

Spiritual blindness is a grave thing. Just like a blind man, he feels his way around. He's never sure of his surroundings, unaware of the goings on around him. Change can occur and not be detected. Evil can be around and there be no awareness. Danger can be around and there be no awareness.

(Then the Lord showed me a campfire in a clearing in the middle of a dark forest at night. The campfire was on the left and I saw many trees to the right. I saw various wild animals lurking around the fire but, not getting very close. Then I saw many ravenous wild animals roaming throughout the trees. I saw myself standing in the middle of the fire. I knew the fire was the Spirit of God)

Wild animals encircle your fire and roam there. But they know better than to get close. They fear, but out in that darkness they roam. The trees are the people among the darkness. There, they can be ravaged. There, they can be attacked. They have no protection! If they would only run to the fire they would be purified and then have the protection they need. Spiritual blindness keeps them from seeing this. (Is. 42:16)

Now Let's Laugh A Little

(I saw the whole story play out between God and this anxious squirrel))

There was this little squirrel. He was extremely anxious. He flitted here, and he flitted there. He really seemed to be quite a nervous kind of guy. Then one day, I put my foot down in his path. He came up curiously enough and checked out my foot. Then he bit me on the foot! "My, why did he do this?" I said to myself. Then I knew why. This squirrel was so used to going about with no one stopping him, to remind him of the really important things. He got very disturbed.

This is like unto my people for they too are used to going about in such a frenzy that when I put my foot out to slow them down, they get angry. They do not see that this block is of me. They truly do not recognize that which I have placed in their path. (Ezek. 20:21)

Pressed Down

(I saw a bowl of dough and saw the thumb of God press down on the dough then, the dough rose up again)

Press down on the dough. See, it surely rises up again. This is what I do unto my people. For when they are pressed, they shall rise up even greater than before. They shall rise up and many shall see them rise up. They shall withstand the fire and shall be baked until they are golden brown. For then, their flavor shall be enjoyed by all. (Ps.145:14)

The Latter Rain

(I heard rain and saw the flowers)

Do you hear the rain? The Latter rain? It's refreshing. All of my beautiful flowers need this latter rain. The new growth needs this latter rain. You will see all the things grow. It will be in full bloom. Then, an angel of God will come and pick all the fully bloomed flowers. They will be ready for the banquet table. (Ps 103:15, Matt 24:31, James 5:7)

My Tools

(I saw a set of tools)

Do you see those tools? Those are my tools. I use them always. I use the gifts of the Spirit. I use the power of My Word. I use the fruit of the Spirit. So, see? I use tools just as you do. Use my tools for fixing what's wrong. For my tools are the best. They are like unto the Craftsman. They have a lifetime guarantee! (1Peter 4:10)

We have a Choice

(I saw an orangutan and saw this whole scenario played out)

I saw a monkey and the Lord said to the monkey, "Will you do as I ask?" The monkey shook his head, no. The Lord asked again, "Will you do as I ask?" The monkey, again, shook his head, no. Then, I saw the monkey picking lice from his head and eating it. Then the Lord spoke to the monkey again. He said, I have created you to swing from the trees and pick bananas from the trees to eat." Then the Lord said, "Will you do as I ask?" The monkey just sat there and shook his head, no. Then, I saw the monkey He laid dead and the lice that the monkey had been feeding upon were now feeding upon the monkey.

(I was impressed that what the monkey had been partaking of in the world, ended up consuming him) (1 John 2:15, Col 3:6)

The Phone Call

One afternoon I was praying in tongues for quite some time. Suddenly, I saw these numbers and I started repeating the numbers in English. I wrote them in my journal and continued praying in tongues. My eyes kept being drawn to the numbers that I had written in the journal and I realized that it was a telephone number. I pondered on it for a few moments to whether I would call the number to see who would answer. I finally took a step of faith and called. A secretary answered and gave the name of a church which I cannot recall. I told her my name and that I had been praying for some time and got this number while I was praying. She became very interested and insisted that the pastor come to the phone. Once the pastor came to the phone, we exchanged pleasantries and he explained a situation at his church that he would like me to pray about. I agreed and made a covenant to pray for his church in Weatherford Texas. To this day I still pray for this pastor and his church.

I have enjoyed this wonderful life learning and seeing through the eyes of the Holy Spirit. At times I ponder on all the possibilities that we have been given access to. I think how short we fall because we do not tap into the great wealth of the Holy Spirit. My pray is that God will never cease to amaze me, and that I will always have an open and willing heart to join Him in any endeavor He chooses.

Surely goodness and mercy shall follow me All the days of my life;
And I will dwell in the house of the Lord Forever. (ps. 23:6)

Here are some scriptures in the Bible of people that experienced visions.

1. Abraham-Gen. 15:1
2. Jacob-Gen. 42:2-4
3. Balaam-Num. 24:2-9
4. Samuel-1Sam. 3:2-15
5. Nathan-2Sam. 7:4, 1Chron. 17:1-15, Ps. 89:19
6. Micaiah-1Kings 22:17-23
7. Daniel-almost all Dan. Ch. 17-12
8. Ananias-Acts 9:10-11
9. Saul/Paul-Acts 9:11-12, 16:9-10, 18:9-10, 22:17-21, 2Cor 12:1-4
10. Cornelius-Acts 10:3-6
11. Peter-Acts 10:9-17, Acts 11:5-10

CHAPTER 14

Evidence That God Calls Us Friend

No longer do I call you servants, for a servant does not know what his master is doing; but I have called you friends, for all things that I heard from My Father I have made known to you. (John 15:15)

There are times that I think the Lord does things just because He is a friend. How amazing is that? A great God, creator of all things, calls us friend. Jesus says He makes known what the Father has shown Him because we are now friends instead of slaves. I think this is incredible and no matter how insignificant we may feel He sees us differently. In one's lifetime, you may consider only a handful of people to be friends. That is a special class of people and for Jesus to place us into that category is exceedingly extraordinary. There are times when I have felt that the Lord told me something, simply, because we are friends. He does not have to tell us what He is doing, yet He does. He likes to fellowship with us and as the scripture above says we are treated like a friend. His purposes are often quite extensive, but I often see them as quite simple. He merely wants to be our friend. Over the years, I have experienced a rich friendship with the Lord. He is the one that began to show me how pertinent and easy it was. As both of us reciprocate in the friend relationship it becomes as real as an earthly friendship. There are a few stories I want to share that showed me evidence that the Lord is a friend.

One time I kept having this strong desire to buy my older brother a lawn mower. Now, I don't usually buy my brother gifts and certainly not something of this sort. I knew he was having trouble with his lawn mower and I could not get it out of my mind to buy him one. After a couple of weeks, I saw one on sale, so I went out and bought it. I took it to my brother on Saturday and told him that I was impressed that God wanted me to buy him this lawnmower. My brother was very pleased and most grateful. I was not for sure if he really believed that the Lord told me to buy it or not, but that did not matter.

On the following Monday I was out doing errands and I kept having this strong feeling that I was going to get a check in the mail. I was thinking God was going to bless me because I was obedient in buying the lawnmower for my brother. I was not expecting any money for any reason, but I continued to have this sense that I would receive a check **that day** in the mail. When I got home from running my errands I could hardly wait to get to the mailbox. I got my mail and opened each piece. THERE IT WAS, a check from the electric company for three dollars more than what I paid for the lawn mower. That was so unbelievable to think my friend, Jesus, had given me the knowing that I was going to get that money. It was fun knowing and expecting such a surprise for the entire day. It was remarkable as I came home and received it just as the Holy Spirit was revealing to me. I firmly believe the Lord does that because He is our friend, He is my Friend! Yes, money comes sometimes because of our obedience, but when He told me that I was going to get money in the mail that showed me the actions of a friend. Friends sometimes cannot wait to tell you something!

Once I woke up in the middle of the night to go to the restroom which is very much a routine these days. I am sleepily walking, and out of the blue, I hear, "Shirley!" I responded, "Yes Lord?" And then I hear, "I love you!" I was startled by His suddenness in the middle of the night. I was extremely groggy and still half asleep as He called out my name. He did that just because He is a friend and more than that He loves me. He truly wants us to know how much He loves each of us. Sometimes, in the still of the night is the best time to hear the Lord. I was so surprised that the Lord addressed me by calling my name. I was even more surprised that I knew immediately that it was the Lord's voice and that I instantly answered Him. He is my friend!

During the weekend of my daughter's wedding I woke up with a major problem with my right eye. It looked all red and looked like pink eye. I put drops in it and placed cold ice on it because not only was it red, but it was swollen. I could not believe, of all times, that this would happen to me. The reception dinner was the next night, and from the look of things I was going to be a hideous sight. I was pouring out my heart to my husband about my eye and how I could not believe the timing of this. My husband turned to me and emphatically said, "Do you really believe, with the close relationship you have with the Lord, that He is going to let you look like that for your daughter's wedding?" His words hit me square in the head. I got such a revelation of that close friendship with the Lord and responded, "You're right, He won't!"

The very next night for the reception dinner my eye was as clear as could be. The following day was the wedding and my eye looked perfectly fine with no recognizable signs of the infection. He is my friend and what an amazing friend He is! Thanks for the **Perfect timing Jesus!** Do you remember a time when Jesus showed you, He was a friend to you?

Once my mother told me she was at a local farm picking strawberries. She said there was a woman with her grandson picking alongside her. Mom said she was thinking that if the little boy was good his grandma was going to take him to get some ice cream. Promptly, as soon as she thought this the boy's grandmother says to him, "Now, if you are a good boy today, I'm going to take you to get an ice cream." I remember my mom telling me that God told her that for no other reason except that He calls us friend. Just like you and I would tell a friend something, so does our Lord.

*And the Scripture was fulfilled which says, "Abraham
believed God, and it was accounted to him for righteousness."
And he was called the friend of God. (James 2:23)*

When I was attending college, I had to go to a get together that my professor was holding in her home. I had stopped off at the college library to pick up a 33-record album for a lesson I was going to teach. That really tells my age! I searched shelf after shelf and I could not locate the record album I needed, and I was going to be late for the party if I did not find it soon. Now, there are two sides to the four rows each of record albums. Records are very thin and difficult to read titles on the edges and they were not organized alphabetically. It was a massive task to locate the one album I needed. I needed it, now, so I wouldn't be late and so I wouldn't have to make another trip back to the university library. I instantly stopped and prayed, "Lord, help me find that album!" I literally turned around, reached my hand toward the shelf and pulled out the exact album I had been feverishly looking for. WOW! I was blown away! The Lord had me literally turn and put my hand on the exact album needed. I still don't comprehend it! He did that because we are friends and He certainly cares about the smallest things in our lives. I love the evidence of His friendship!

The Lord cares so much about us because we are His creation, His children, and His friend. There was a major thing that the Lord did for my dad and it really showed me how much He cares.

One night at midnight I got an unexpected phone call. I heard someone on the other end of the line which was quite disturbing. I heard someone calling for help in a weak and panicked voice. As I listened carefully, I realized it was my dad. Apparently, he had the phone turned upside down and was speaking into the ear part. He was calling out for someone to help him. He was saying that he fell. I responded over and over to let him know I was on my way. To no avail, he could not hear my words. I immediately woke my husband up and we promptly drove down to my dad's house. I unlocked the door with the house key and began calling out to my dad. It was dark throughout the whole house. As I entered the bedroom, there was my dad. He had fallen and was not able to get up. He kept frantically asking, "How did you know?" I said, "Dad, you called me!"

Once we got him up in his bed, and he calmed down, we realized he was not seriously injured. He had been on the floor for five hours. He had fallen after getting up and out of his bed. He explained that he had taken his cane and knocked the phone off the table and pulled it to himself and started punching buttons, after realizing he was not able to get up. He, miraculously, must have pushed the redial button to call back the last person he had called because I was the last person my dad talked to earlier that day. I was astonished! There is no way my dad dialed the number because he always looked up numbers in his little brown book. He did not remember anyone's number, anyway. Besides he had the phone upside down and he did not know how I knew he had fallen. Isn't God Good? Not only did he care so much for my father, but he allowed me to be the one to get the call to go help him. God is truly my friend and I was truly grateful.

Know that God is with you, and His character is as a friend.

One Saturday morning years ago, I had heard about an art exhibit at the Holiday Inn. I loved oil painting, so I strolled into the exhibit and walked about for a very long time gazing upon all the beautiful artwork. I only had so much money and realized I could buy a painting but the picture frame to go with it cost twenty-five dollars. There was no need to purchase a picture without the frame, although I continued to look and look. There sure were some beautiful paintings in there and I had never bought artwork painted by an artist before. I finally spied out the one I would buy if I bought one. It was a beautiful snow scene of mountains in beautiful blues and whites. It was so pretty.

Eventually, I decided that I would not buy the picture because I didn't have enough money. I left disappointed and walked back to my car. As I got right up to my car, I saw something right by the door of my car. It looked like money folded up. I reached down and unfolded a twenty and a five equaling the exact amount of money I needed to buy the frame for that beautiful picture. I was so touched, and I knew 100% that the Lord placed that money there for that picture frame. I let out a great big, "Thank You Lord!" My heart was so touched realizing what He had just done.

Of course, I ran straight back into the hotel and grabbed the picture and watched as they assembled the frame for the oil painting. What a blessing! I know that sounds like such a small thing, but when you realize that a great big God cares about your heart's desire, it is quite humbling. I still have that oil painting hanging in my basement and it is my evidence that God is my friend.

Again, just Last night, while planning a day trip with my aunt the Lord showed me that He is a friend. He is my friend! When He gives me evidence of His friendship the feeling is indescribable. It touches me tremendously in ways that I may not completely understand. My question is why such a Great God would care that much about one person. Out of all the people that ever lived why take notice of one tiny detail? All I can attribute it to is that God has such great love. Sometimes I can't fathom the extent of His love. I know that all things are possible for those who believe thus we couldn't possibly be believing big enough!

> *Jesus said to him, "If you can believe,[a] all things are*
> *possible to him who believes." (Mark 9:23)*

My aunt and I spend every Thursday together and we were trying to come up with something to do. Sometimes we do work, but often we play, and we had decided to do a short, day trip. She suggested a place we had gone with my daughters two years ago that my sister-in-law told us about.

So, I texted my sister-in-law and tried to jar her memory of the place we wanted to go. Silly as it is, it was a thrift store. I continued to describe the possible location, so she gave me a place in French Lick. When I told my aunt, she informed me that it wasn't French Lick. She is right like that! I then just stopped and said, "Lord, where was that thrift store?" Immediately, I saw in a vision the restaurant "The Schnitzelbank" and then I saw down the street. This place was down the street from the Schnitzelbank restaurant!

My first words were, "Thank You, Lord!"

I grabbed the computer and looked up the restaurant on the internet and realized that it was in Jasper. After that, I searched for all thrift stores in Jasper and there it was. When I saw the picture online, I could tell that it was on the same street as the restaurant.

Today we drove over an hour to go to lunch and to go to that thrift store. It was right down the street from the restaurant just like the vision showed.

What an amazing Friend!

CHAPTER 15

Evidence That God Restores

And the God of all grace, who called you to his eternal glory in
Christ, after you have suffered a little while, will himself restore
you and make you strong, firm and steadfast. (1 Peter 5:10)

Many years ago, while praying I saw in a vision a nest with three eggs in it. A snake slithered in and began to take one of the eggs. I knew this was a warning and I immediately knew this was about my children. The three eggs were my three children and the egg that was being stolen by the snake was my youngest daughter, Sara

That day forward I increasingly prayed that the snake would not steal any of my children. My children belonged to God and the enemy was not having even one. Because of the vision I prayed more extensively for Sara. Not only did I pray for her protection, but I also guarded her, to some extent, from the world. She was not allowed to run around outside as much, and I did not let her spend the night with others as much as her brother. I prayed for all my children's friends and I prayed for any neighbors when they moved into the neighborhood to be good for my children. I thought I covered every area!

All seemed great with Sara throughout the years. She was a sweet child and was very giving. If I gave her any money, she would always share it with someone else, but primarily with her brother. She was very generous and joined me in ministry helping with setting up for meetings and running the overhead for the worship time.

She was a giggly girl, yet somewhat quiet and was very sincere. She brought a lot of joy to our family. Sara had always been in sports playing baseball and loved it. By the time she was in high school her focus was on basketball. Sara was rather tall and had beautiful long blond hair with the cutest dimples when she smiled. As the years went by, she excelled at basketball and became the starting center for her high school team. Life could not have been better for her and for the whole family.

During a crisis in the family, things turn in a completely different direction. I had been flying back and forth from Florida helping with my brother that was in a coma. We were trying to keep at least one family member there to be with him. Upon returning from one of my trips I found that Sara had quit the basketball team. She had found someone of ill reputation and was falling in love in the worst way. She completely abandoned her Christian upbringing and abandoned her dreams of playing basketball in college. One day all seemed perfect, and the next day we were not sure who she was or even **where** she was.

It was a horrifying experience! We were not even sure what was happening at first. Then we found out that drugs were involved and that took us all to places no one ever wants to go. She was not coming home, she quit school, and basketball was over! Then not long after that we were getting calls from the police. It was just unimaginable and my husband and myself were broken hearted. We were terrified and downright scared. We tried everything! I even, had the women in the family try an intervention. I drove the van and me, my other daughter, and my mother all met her in a parking lot and tried to talk to her. We said everything we could possibly think of, but she would not listen. This was way bigger than any of us! Absolutely nothing was working to help resolve this ordeal. Help from God was the only way this travesty was ever going to change. It was messy and our whole family felt on the brink of destruction over this. Believe me, it was worse than anyone could imagine. It got to the point that I didn't know if she was going to make it out alive. The worst possible drugs were involved and with drugs comes criminal behavior. Our eyes were opened to a whole different world. The world only seen on TV or somewhere far away! Yes, our whole country is experiencing this horrid epidemic of drug addiction and we experienced it firsthand.

Sara's personality completely changed. It was unlike anything I had ever seen! She was argumentative and hateful and had become impossible to talk to. Her boyfriend was so controlling that it was impossible to spend any time with her without nonstop phone call interruptions from him. Between the boyfriend, drug addiction, and the horrifying lifestyle I felt like she was slipping away. For the first time in my life I felt completely incapacitated and unable to help in any way. I had fought for her, prayed for her, and cried for her! This went on for several years and all I could do now was stand in faith and hold on to God. He was our only hope!

Therefore, take up the whole armor of God, that you may be able to withstand in the evil day, and having done all, to stand. (Eph 6:13)

Out of my sheer desperation I made a phone call and spoke at length to a woman from a drug treatment center. Thanks be to God! She stated that my daughter needed a longer treatment care placement and she recommended the Healing Place in Louisville Kentucky. What a God send!!!

The following week I talked Sara into going to the Healing Place. I told her I could no longer help her and that she was not able to even help herself. Reluctantly, she went. She spent a year there and did very well, so I thought. It was not long after getting out of the treatment center when she began to slip back into the drug lifestyle. Except for this time, because of the program's teachings, she had a harder time having as much fun out on the streets. She always knew about God but did not really know Him. She had received Jesus in her life as a child and had also been filled with the Holy Spirit. She was raised in a strong Christian home with plenty of fun and lots of love. All the assurances seemed to be there! But then, here she was fighting for her life. We were ALL fighting for her life!

I was completely confused! I had prayed everything that there was to pray as she was growing up! I was also frustrated because I saw the nest and saw the snake going in to steal her in that vision and so… what was the purpose of **knowing that** if it was going to happen anyway? I needed answers but was not getting them. Why didn't my prayers keep this from happening? Honestly, for the first time in my life, my faith was very low. We had seven deaths in the family within a three-year span, and It had zapped nearly all my spiritual energy. However, my love and close relationship with the Lord never wavered and I never felt angry toward God.

It was now seven years into a total nightmare when my friend and I were praying together in the car. We were getting ready to go visit at a women's prison. While sitting in the car my thoughts are raging and I am thinking in my head, that someday, I could be visiting my own daughter here! What an awful thought! I was prepared for that, but I did not want that for her or our family.

We had the **GREAT I AM,** and it was not supposed to be like this!

My friend and I had been discussing my daughter and then began to pray. At the end of our praying a song kept going through my head over and over. Just then, my friend looks up at me with tears in her eyes and says, "I've got a feeling everything is going to be alright!" I could not believe it! That is exactly the song that was running through my head, so I began to sing, "I've got a feelin….everythings gonna be alright!" Then we both began to sing it! "I've got a feelin….everythings gonna be alright!"

From that point on, in my heart, I knew God was saying everything **was** going to be alright. I was grateful for that word that day from the Lord. The confirmation from my friend let me really know that God was taking care of my daughter. It was His word of encouragement in an extremely dark time.

Shortly thereafter, Sara went back into the Healing Place and spent another year there, all the while, growing spiritually in God. Step by step, day by day things got better and better. Then one day, I was in the car talking to the Lord. The car is a great meeting place with God for me. Seems like quite a few spiritual experiences have happened in the car. On that day something rose up in me and I began calling out to the Lord! I began to ask God for Sara. I began to tell Him I wanted her. I wanted her to be by my side like it was with my mother. I cried out loudly, "Give her to me!" "I want Sara!" I told Him I wanted to be in ministry with her and for her to be by my side. It was like a wave of the Holy Spirit boldness came on me. Again, I felt an assurance that everything was going to be alright. I knew God had heard me and I knew it was by His Spirit that I even asked for such a thing with such tenacity.

It was not long after that when I started hearing Sara talk about God in an intimate way. She began to enter worship and experience His presence. She started praying for girls at the Healing Place. I started hearing the girls from the healing place call Sara an inspiration to them. I literally saw God restore my daughter. She had gone through a remarkable program, but I could see Him sealing her and marking her for Himself. I saw Him setting her aside for His glory. Not only did He restore her, but He restored her back to me, back to our family. It has been over three years and the turnaround has been remarkable. Her heart has been restored, her faith has been restored, and her whole life is being blessed.

She just got married to a wonderful Christian man and just bought a new home. She works in a place where she drug tests women, teaches classes on addiction and is involved with a Christian recovery group called Celebrate Recovery. Through her job she was just given a case load at the Healing Place as peer support ministering to women, just like herself. She is helping them come out of addiction. She has the freedom to give God glory, publicly, for what He has done, and she gets to teach others about the delivering power of Jesus. Remember the thoughts I had while sitting in the car before going into prison? Well, Sara is going to prison! She goes with me to solitary confinement and minister's life to women in need of hope. So many of the girls in prison are close to her age and they are inspired by her encouragement. I can see it in their eyes. Sara looks at those girls and realizes that it could have been her on the other side of that cell. We are all forever grateful! Glory be to His Holy name! He truly does bring good out of dreadful circumstances just as it says. This is the greatest evidence that God restores!

And we know that all things work together for good to those who love God, to those who are the called according to His purpose. (Romans 8:28)

I just shake my head, with a great big smile, in amazement at what God has done. You never know how grateful you become over something precious you have… until you almost lose it. By the way, I do not question any more. But, I still think about that nest and the eggs and that evil one that came to steal, kill and destroy and I know for certain….without God, without His wisdom, things could have been a whole lot worse! God Wins!

CHAPTER 16

Evidence That God Gives Dreams

And it shall come to pass in the last days, says God, That I will pour out of My Spirit on all flesh; Your sons and your daughters shall prophesy, your young men shall see visions, your old men shall dream dreams. Acts 2:17

I believe the body of Christ is in her finest hour of receiving from God. God's children have been equipped to prophesy and to have dreams and visions. This promise for the last days is important. The Church needs everything the Holy Spirit provides for empowerment. Expect it! You don't have to be old nor do you have to be a man to dream dreams. This statement from acts is conveying that we should all expect these encounters and acknowledge them. I have been blessed and encouraged by dreams from God. We must wake up, fully, to what God is doing to move in unity with Him. We are spirit beings living in a natural world. The more we encounter the ways of God's Holy Spirit the more we will understand how His kingdom works.

In the mid-eighties I saw, in a dream, the bride of Christ. I saw a woman in a bridal gown lying at the foot of a garbage heap sound asleep. There was a bulldozer coming in and removing all the garbage from around her. Then, I saw the Lord's huge hands scoop her up and as He did this, she slowly woke up and yawned. When she was stretching and yawning, I noticed she had dirt smudges on her face and on her bridal gown. I saw the Lord begin to clean the smudges off her with His fingers and then, I woke up.

This dream caused me to begin to pray for the bride of Christ. It made me very focused on seeking God for wisdom for the body of believers. Since He focused on the body of Christ so did I. I still pray for Him to wake us up and clean us up! That dream reminds me of what God is doing with us and is a great illustration. I pray that God will remove us from all that garbage as we are being prepared for Him.

> *Husbands, love your wives, even as Christ also loved the church, and*
> *gave himself for it; That he might sanctify and cleanse it with the*
> *washing of water by the word, that He might present it to himself*
> *a glorious church, not having spot, or wrinkle, or any such thing;*
> *but that it should be holy and without blemish. Eph 5:25-27*

There are purposes for all dreams God gives, but not all dreams are a message from Him. I have found that if it is Him giving the message there is clarity in its understanding. Although, sometimes we don't have the complete revelation of a God dream, but as we seek the Lord for the revelation, He will be faithful to give it. Most of my God dreams seem to be for prayer. There are some of my dreams given that serve as warnings or for direction. Some are for prophetic insight or revelation. God sent dreams to people throughout the Bible and it makes for a good study.

Once I dreamed all night long before going to a funeral and dinner at my cousins. I woke up throughout the night dreaming that I stood up in the middle of all my extended family members and told them about receiving Jesus. The focal point of the dream kept hitting on the point that we were all going to take a turn. Just like the man that had died, we too, would take our turn. During the repeated dream I led the whole family in a prayer to receive Christ as Savior. I dreamed this probably five times and then I could not get it out of my mind each time I would awaken. I had never had anything like this to happen to me and I felt very sure that this was something the Lord was wanting me to do.

The next day, I was physically shaken at knowing what I was to do that day. Honestly, I was a nervous wreck. I knew this side of the family well, but I did not see them often. It was not my nature to preach at family members and I am a little reserved when I have not been around people in a while. I kept thinking and wondering why I would need to do such a drastic thing during a time to be reverent to the deceased and his family. Believe me, I was trying to think of many reasons not to do this! I knew for certain the Lord wanted me to follow the dream as He showed me, and I needed to be obedient.

After everyone was finishing a nice meal, I knew it was time. I was very nervous as I got up and asked my cousin if I could say something. She said that I could. I began to explain how I normally did not do something such as this, but that I had dreams all night long about getting up before them. I went on with the message about the family member that just left us and then emphasized that we were all going to **take a turn** just as he had. My voice was shaking, and I felt uneasy. I told them in the dream that I had prayed a prayer with them to receive Jesus and I was going to do that. I told them that they needed to be ready when it was their turn. Then I told them that if they wanted to pray with me that they could. It was so quiet that you could hear a pin drop in that room! I prayed aloud before over twenty of my family members.

No one prayed out loud except me and it was extremely quiet for the next few minutes. Several family members came up and thanked me for doing what I did. I do not have a clue who the prayer was for that day, but I knew what I was supposed to do. Since then, several of those family members have **taken their turn** and I pray they were ready.

I have found that God does not always tell us the details in all that He is doing nor does He have to explain Himself. I have a good feeling that, somehow, we would mess things up if we knew too much concerning a matter. All I know is that He wants us to be obedient to what He calls us to do. If we continue to be obedient, whether we see results or not, He will bless us as we are faithful. It is very difficult to be obedient when God asks us to do something that is not in our nature. We might even feel foolish or feel incompetent to do the task. As we are obedient to the best of our ability God will work out the details. In this case the dream was to carry out a task.

You would think He would give you a dream because you have reached a place in your life of greater spirituality, but I have not found that to be true. One of the most exciting dreams I have ever had was when I was first married, and I had only been a Christian for a couple of years. I was mad at my husband and shamefully I was taking the alternate place to sleep, the couch! Unexpectedly and undeserving... the dream came.

In my dream I was standing at the edge of a vast sea and it was at night. There were two large, glowing stone pillars, one on each side of me. I proceeded to walk out into the sea about waist deep. As I stood there, I felt the most glorious presence of the Lord. It was as if waves of increasing glory swept over me. With each wave it intensified. I have felt His presence before and surely it is wonderful, but this was nothing I had ever experienced before.

As this feeling of intense anointing peaked, I turned around and there was Jesus sitting on a smaller stone pillar. He was wearing a white robe and the whole place seemed to have an iridescent, white, bright light. I could not make out Jesus' facial features. His whole head emanated with white light. I saw ticker taped words running across His forehead and on the bottom of His robe. I was straining to read all the words. I remember reading, "Lord of Lords and King of Kings" and then I woke up. I was ecstatic! I had seen Jesus and felt Him in a remarkable way! I promptly went in the bedroom and told my husband I had seen Jesus in a dream.

These will make war with the Lamb, and the Lamb will overcome them, for He is Lord of lords and King of kings; and those who are with Him are called, chosen, and faithful." (Rev. 17:14)

I thought about every detail of the dream and what it conveyed. Since I struggled with reading the ticker taped scripture, I felt like one revelation of the dream was that I was struggling with reading His word. It caused me to press into His Word and pray that I would hunger for His word. As I walked into the water waist deep, I am reminded of the scripture in Ezekiel. The deeper we go with the Lord shows our surrender to Him. The Lord's presence kept increasing in the dream as He got closer. That was amazing to feel the closeness. I have often thought that maybe we would feel His presence more intensely the closer it came for Him to return.

Sometimes Jesus just wants to reveal Himself to us. When Jesus appeared to me in that dream, I was elated, but I remembered feeling saddened because the first time I saw Jesus I was on the couch because I was angry at my husband. Did He do that on purpose?

Again, he measured one thousand and brought me through the waters; the water came up to my knees. Again, he measured one thousand and brought me through; the water came up to my waist. (Ezek 47:4)

Jesus communicates to anyone He chooses by dreams, including children. I have seen this on occasion with my own children. He wants to teach them also about who He is and what His kingdom is about. Your children are never too young to receive a revelation from Jesus. My daughter had a very interesting dream when she was very small. I have never forgotten it.

In her dream Jesus revealed salvation's process. The dream began with a woman holding a baby in her arms. She was going down a creek jumping from one stone to another. There were people on both sides of the creek, and they were clapping their hands and cheering her on, "Come on, you can do it!" Upon hearing this the woman would leap to another rock and then to another rock getting her farther down through the creek. The people all continued to cheer her on when, suddenly, the woman walked up a set of steps and went through the doors of a church.

That is a perfect illustration of how the body of Christ is supposed to encourage people. As we encourage and direct people, they gladly enter God's kingdom. It takes the whole body to do this. I think the Lord wanted to show my daughter a visual detailing her part to lead people to Jesus. He wanted to teach her the joy of salvation for the believer and the body of believers. God is no respecter of persons. He delights in revealing Himself and His kingdom principles to His children. Sara was around eight years old and was so excited when she told me about her dream. Without my help she had a good understanding what God was showing her and what the dream was conveying.

My son also had an impactful dream as a young boy. The dream was prophetic and was fulfilled later in his life.

He dreamed that he had a ring and had lost it. He looked everywhere for the ring and was very upset because he lost it. When my son finally found his ring, it was broken. He took the ring to Jesus and handed it to Him. Jesus took the ring and when He handed it back to Phillip it was repaired, it was restored. Phillip was very happy when Jesus fixed his ring.

I remember the morning my son had this dream. He ran to me with such excitement that Jesus had fixed his ring! I recorded it in a journal. Later in years as Phillip became a young man he strayed from the Lord. He had broken covenant relationship with the Lord. We were at church where our pastor preached a sermon about this ring and how we break covenant with the Lord. It was remarkable to the similarities between the dream and the sermon. My son and I discussed it all the way home from church. We both recognized it was in direct relationship to Phillip's dream. The most incredible aspect of the dream was that Jesus fixed this broken ring. He was restoring the broken covenant between Him and my son. The pastor's whole sermon perfectly matched the situation. My son had just come back to the Lord and Jesus was restoring him to Himself. He repaired the ring! Just like in a marriage, the wedding ring symbolizes a covenant between two people. It was not until that message came from the pastor did we have the complete revelation of that dream.

My oldest daughter, Amy, had a dream that the Lord was holding her heart in His hand and all these people were jumping up trying to get at it. We both understood that the dream meant that Jesus was going to hold her heart and protect it from others. This meant a lot to Amy to know that the Lord was encouraging her of this. If your children have spiritual dreams, take them seriously. Allow them to retell as many details as they are able to remember. Record their dreams for them to let them know God's dreams are valuable.

I have had several evangelistic dreams where I am leading groups of people to the Lord. They are very energizing, but none as thrilling as a dream I had a few years ago. I dreamed I was attending a huge Bible study in a cafeteria. When I packed up my belongings and began to exit the meeting, I heard a commotion across the room. A friend of mine was standing and yelling across the room. Two men were trying to get her to sit down and be quiet. They were taking their hands pushing her back. She continued to yell and anxiously points at me from across the room. She emphatically yelled, "I need to talk to Shirley Hall!" "I need to talk to Shirley Hall about God!"

The dream then transitioned into another scene. In this next scene, I found myself in a room where I was waiting to talk to this woman about God. As I walked over to the window, I saw the most horrific storm I had ever seen. There were the blackest clouds and the most turbulence I had ever seen in the sky. As she arrived, I looked at her and told her there was no place to hide. We then began to search for some place to get shelter from that horrific storm. As we frantically looked around there was nowhere to hide to get away from the storm. At that point I woke up.

I was certain this was a dream from the Lord, and I felt an expectancy that the Lord was about to do something. I felt like this woman was going to go through a great storm in her life. That morning when I arrived at work, I saw this person from the dream in the hall. Laughingly, I told her that I had a dream about her. She responded with something humorous. Later that day we ended up sitting beside each other during lunch. She turned to me and asked about the dream. I told her I would not be able to explain right then, but that she could stop by my room on break and I would tell her about the dream. For some reason she never showed up to hear about the dream that day.

The next morning, I saw her again. She eagerly remarked that she wanted to hear all about the dream and that she would see me at our next break. Later that day she arrived at my room and I told her the entire dream. I did not really know exactly what to say, so I questioned her if she really did want to know about God. Moments later, she broke down crying and told me that something had been bothering her. She said she had been talking to her friends about an incident that had just occurred with her son. She seemed amazed at the coincidence. She confided that the other day she was in the kitchen with her son and that she had made some sort of comment about God to him. She said the look on her son's face told her he did not have a clue what she was talking about. She had a sudden realization that she had gone to church when she was younger, but her son did not have a clue about anything concerning God. She had not taught him anything about God and it extremely saddened her. In the end, she prayed to receive Christ. I also prayed for her concerning several details from the dream.

We never know what is going on in people's lives, but God does. He orchestrated the entire event for multiple purposes. It was His desire to touch my friend and therefore used a dream to accomplish it. I do not know all that was achieved through that dream, but I know God loves each of us so much that He will send whatever necessary to relay His message. Not only does He encourage us, but He instills hope. I give Him all the glory!

The power of dreams can be life changing!

We are being transformed by the renewing of our minds, by the Word of God. His Word can come in the form of a dream today! Be ready to value God's dreams. Be ready to record them. Be ready to respond to them. Be ready to impart the wisdom from them.

Awhile back I had a dream of the coming of the Lion of Judah. I have titled it for easy reference.

Lion of Judah

I walked into a house and I was aware it had spiritual people in it. I looked in the front room and saw three girls sitting on a couch laughing, talking and goofing off. I walked into the living room to find a man and a woman sitting on the couch. I began to introduce myself and told them my testimony about when I received Christ into my life. The woman jumped up and began to tell me how this man she was with had been touched by the power of God. As I was listening intently the man stood up and walked over to me and took my left hand. Immediately I felt a surge of power that convinced me that God had surely touched him. A strong power ran up my arm to my elbow. By this time, I had fallen to the floor and was lying there thinking about how my whole arm was tingling with this surge of power. A strong thought came to me. I kept hearing the words, unless it be to the glory of God...it is for nothing. I spoke these words aloud to myself three times.

The next scene I was asleep, lying on my back, on a couch in a back room of this same house. I was so sound asleep when a dark-haired little boy came right over the top of me and within inches of my face said loudly, "Come and See!" I was so groggy and saw him in clouded vision. I mistakenly said, "Ok Nathaniel" Again he repeated loudly, "Come and See!" I quickly corrected myself as I awoke because I heard emphatically from within that this is not Nathaniel...This was David! I said sleepily, "Oh, okay David" and I got up to go with him. He took me out of the back door to the outside and it was at night.

He pointed up to the sky and said, "Look!" I looked up and all the stars had gathered together and formed a lion's head. David said, "Look, it is the Lion of Judah and He is coming!" As he pointed to the right of the stars he said, "The saints are on His right." Then pointing to the left side of the Lion's head formed from the stars, David said, "And the righteous are by His side." I then thought in amazement, what an awesome sight this was to see!

At that time, two girls were coming out of the house talking and laughing and just being social as the girls on the inside had been. I yelled to them to get their attention toward the sky and exclaimed, "Look up there!" They nonchalantly looked up, and then with no reaction or response walked on their way.

I then woke up. I knew immediately by the Spirit of God that the girls were the foolish virgins. I also knew that the boy was King David as a child awakening me to the knowledge of Jesus' second coming. He is the Lion of Judah. The three girls in the house plus the two girls outside just laughing and goofing off symbolized the five foolish virgins. I understood that the man that touched me, presumably by the power of God, was not necessarily so.

I used that dream to pray for the body of Christ, but primarily I used it for teaching. God wants us to be prepared for His coming. He wants us to be filled with the oil which represents the Holy Spirit. The Bible states that Jesus' coming will be like a thief in the night. We will not know the day or the hour He comes. I also was amazed that the same words, come and see, are repeated several times in the book of Revelation.

*Now I saw when the Lamb opened one of the seals; and
I heard one of the four living creatures saying with a
voice like thunder, "Come and see."(Rev 6:1)*

But one of the elders said to me, "Do not weep. Behold, the
Lion of the tribe of Judah, the Root of David, has prevailed
to open the scroll and to loose its seven seals." (Rev 5:5)

Not all dreams are from the Lord. I have certain criteria in which I
determine the validity for a dream being from God. I look for earmarks
in which show me evidence of being a potential dream from the Lord.
Here is a list I go by.

- I have a strong knowing that it is from God
- It lines up with scripture
- It contains a message
- It gives me wisdom for prayer
- I wake up immediately after the dream
- I hear specific words or have specific thoughts after the dream
- If it warns
- The dream is confirmed

I usually have at least two or more of these earmarks to determine
my confidence of it being from the Lord. If the dream has elements that
I don't completely understand I seek the Lord for wisdom. I always write
the dream down, so I don't lose any parts of the dream or misrepresent the
meaning of the dream. It is very easy to forget details unless you record
them. Nearly all the dreams, visions and stories are written verbatim to the
very best of my ability. I am very particular about not paraphrasing things
the Lord has given me. I value them and would never want to misrepresent
anything He has spoken to me or shown me.

Here is another dream I had approximately thirteen years ago. It is
about the Jewish people and a planned holocaust. All I can say is that
this dream and the one concerning the virgins have caused me to pray,
extensively, for the body of Christ and for the Jewish people. I have also
shared with a few intercessors concerning these two dreams. I may not

have the complete understanding of them, but I have tried to respond to them the best I know how.

Holocaust

I was with my husband in the United States and we were searching for a place to live. We were looking for a place to hide and live. Something had occurred in the United States to cause us to be in this position. We were in a car pulling a camper with all our belongings. Abruptly, our vehicle was stuck in the mud and we were unable to get out of it.

The next scene I am in a completely different setting (not America) with dirt and cobblestones as the streets. It resembled a town in the Middle East. I am an older Jewish woman. I am walking through a street with shops. I am trying to hide my identity as being Jewish. I am looking for a place to live and to hide my family. I have a lengthy scarf draping over my head, and I am trying to hide my face. As I look up, on occasion, I catch the eyes of three different men. They are also Jewish, and they are trying to hide their identity also. They are looking for some place to hide, some place to live unnoticed. I know them, and they know me, that we are Jewish. No one else seems to know our identity.

I walked into a shop and instead of being a shop it is a small museum. It is a museum of past atrocities of the Holocaust. As I walked around the museum, I saw pictures and small items of torture from the holocaust (under Hitler). I noticed that it was minimizing the horrific holocaust of the 1940s by displaying these small items.

I walked out of the museum and looked around as I walked down the street. On the right, I saw an entryway to a very large factory. It looked like it was under some construction. After I took a few steps into the factory I spied a hole in the concrete wall, way in the back in an uninhabited part of the factory. I thought about it as being a hiding place, a place of refuge for my family. I continued to travel throughout this enormous factory. I got to the second floor and I saw in a very large room, two Jewish children being fitted for uniforms and fitted for shoes. They had everything taken from them and they were going to outfit them in these other items of clothing. There was a very large stack of uniforms and special shoes that they were making for the Jews. In the dream I was under the impression that there was another plan of destruction of the Jews. It was going to be on a mass scale of destruction after seeing the various objects being prepared in this factory.

I went to another floor and saw a gigantic area of where they were baking bread. There was freshly baked bread everywhere. The bread was in the ovens, on shelves and on huge trays. No people were around, and It looked as if the day was done for baking bread. The bread was sitting and cooling on racks everywhere. Beyond and off to the back I spy the very same holes in the construction that led to the place I had thought I could bring my family to hide. My next thought was that we would have bread to eat. Then, I woke up.

I knew this was a dream from the Lord.

I wondered all morning, what was God trying to tell me? Then I thought maybe I needed to pray about the Jewish people and about another holocaust being planned against them.

A few hours later, I flip on television and I see John Hagee and he is sitting with a Jewish man having a conversation. They were discussing a possible coming holocaust against God's people and Israel. He was also telling about his new book, *Jerusalem Countdown*. To say the least, I went out and bought the book and began to pray. I gathered with my closest friends, most of which are intercessors in the body of Christ. We had an interesting meeting and prayed for Israel and the Jewish people.

Again, I am not sure of all the details in this dream, but I feel that it is a prophetic dream. I ask you, also, to pray for the Jewish people. Many events are occurring in the world today that point to difficult times ahead. Even we in the United States could be headed for times of trials and tribulation. Please pray! Pray that you and your family will be prepared for the days ahead.

Korea

I had a strange dream around five years ago. I dreamed I was sleeping in a very large warehouse on the floor. It was nighttime and this warehouse was full of people laying asleep everywhere on the floor. I woke up and began to walk to the bathroom. As I walked to the bathroom, I noticed that I had a small white flag in my hand, and I was waving it back and forth all the way to the bathroom. I stopped waving it for a second and turned it to the side and looked at the small white flag. On the flag was written the word, Korea. I continued walking and as I began to enter the bathroom, I heard machine guns going off everywhere outside. We were under attack. I ran into the bathroom and thought I could hide in there and hopefully no one would find me! Then I woke up.

It was a very alarming dream. I was not aware of anything about Korea. Besides, there was a North Korea and a South Korea. I, honestly, did not know exactly how to pray. But I began to pray for safety for these people. Because of the flag I thought it represented surrender because it was white. I began praying, simply, that Korea would surrender since I didn't know which Korea it was. I prayed at length the best of my ability. I continued to look out for some sort of confirmation. Three days later, I read a news article that North Korea attacked some sort of building in South Korea. It did not seem to make much news and I think a couple of people died. That was some confirmation, but often I just pray and go on hearing nothing more.

Now, today, North Korea is very much in the news. They are coming into a position of surrender to the United States and to South Korea. That is exactly the reference from the news. I somehow wonder if this had anything to do with that dream. This is the first time in over fifty years that North and South Korea have even spoken so this is really making the news. My prayer recently concerning the leader, Kim Jong Un, has been one concerning his family. He has always been a brutal dictator killing many of his own people. He has allowed his people to live in devastating situations and many are said to be starving. He has recently gotten married to a beautiful woman and has two very small children. I have been praying that he will have such love for these children that he rethinks taunting the nations around him with war.

Recently, Kim Jong Un has started meeting leaders for peace. I know prayer works! Many pray for our country and our leaders. I also know North Korea's leader might have realized that he and his whole family might be in danger because the United states was very close to bombing them. North Korea has been threatening the United States with nuclear bombs and we were on the brink of war. I also got wind that we might have caused one of their underground missiles to explode and their test site collapsed. God gets all the glory for all He does. And how He does it is sometimes a mystery. I just try to be faithful in the tiny specs I am given.

I had another very strange dream around three years ago. It too was quite disturbing and was very short.

Chinese Architecture

I dreamed I was in New Albany, Indiana. I was exiting the 265 bypass onto the State Street off-ramp. I looked over and could see a zoomed in version of the building I call the Capital Building which is actually the Mercer Building across the river in Louisville, Kentucky. To the immediate right of the Mercer building I saw where a huge Chinese building resembling the Imperial Palace was built. In the dream this building was brought into focus by zooming in on it.

Then I woke up!

I was very disturbed by this dream, and it brought a bit of a gasp. I was seeing something startling being built in my community. My first impression was that China had invaded and they were building in our country. To this day, I continue to look at the area next to the Mercer Building wondering how that could be done. I really believe that someday that spot will be filled with that massive Chinese structure. Recently, I have seen some huge cranes and heavy equipment in the area where I believe could be an area erected for this building. It could possibly be a multicultural building that we build and nothing to be concerned with at all! I looked up a couple of definitions concerning this type of structure on the internet. Here is what I found.

Imperial Palaces

Imperial palaces were originally built to serve the extravagant lifestyles of the emperors, as well as to provide a centralized location for demonstrating imperial political control. The imperial palaces were built on a grand scale, sparing no expense to display the majesty and dignity of the imperial power of the time. Each successive emperor contributed grandeur to the structures, and today, these palaces stand for all to enjoy.

Each imperial palace is a testament to the history and glory of Chinese culture.

This next dream encouraged me to get into the word. It also gave me something to hold onto on that day that I go to be with the Lord. It challenged me to consider the things I am doing and to consider whether they are things that will just pass away or things that will remain because they glorify God.

Meeting on the Hill

I was clinging to the back of a trailer and as it turned a corner something long and sharp pierced me in my left temple. I died because of the accident. The next thing I know is that it is dark, and I am walking up a steep hill. It is very bright at the top of the hill and beyond. As I am walking up the hill, I see my mother and father and I see my husband. They are walking down the hill. Once they got to me, we all turned around to walk back to where they had come from. I joined the right-hand side of my husband and all four of us walked up the hill toward the lighted hilltop

The next scene, I stood by a place where I heard lots of music and people are dancing. I was not allowed to go out where the people were, but I wanted to. There was an indication that I could not join the people dancing because of my body and I understood. At that point, I was escorted by someone. They did not speak but escorted me down many corridors. I heard music the whole time.

Next thing, the escort stopped in front of a door. As soon as I stepped in front of it the door flung open and there was a brilliant light within the room. I went in and walked around to a tall wall inside the room and looked up and all around the wall. There were sticky notes covering the entire wall. Each of the notes had many nice things people had said about me. Once I read most of them, I left the room and was escorted down more corridors. Again, we stopped in front of another door and it too flung open. The brilliance of the room drew me in. In this room there were children sitting everywhere. As I walked by them, they raised their hand and shook my hand and thanked me. I had been a teacher most of my adult life and they were thanking me. Once again, I found myself being escorted back into the music filled hallways. The odd thing was that every corridor was dark. I couldn't see anything and could only hear music except when I was taken to each of these rooms. I did not ever feel afraid because of the darkness and I never could see the person that was escorting me. I do remember thinking how I wanted to remember all that I had seen in each of the rooms. I knew I had visited hundreds of rooms depicting parts of my life. Unfortunately, I could only remember three rooms. The last room I remember going into opened just like the others, and the room was lit up brightly. I walked over to a large podium which contained a very large opened book. I began turning the pages. Many of the pages were empty but some of the pages had scriptures on them. I knew I needed to learn more of the Word, know the Word.

Once again, I was being escorted down more music-filled hallways. As we walked down this one hallway there was another hallway perpendicular to our hallway. It was lit at the end and I craned my neck to see some men escorting Jesus up the hallway. Jesus had a deep, dark red robe on, and He had a stern look on His Face. He was on His way to do something serious. I wanted to stop and get a better look at Jesus, but I was moved on. The escort continued to take me down more corridors wherein I stopped in front of two giant double doors. As I stood there, they flew open. I stood at the threshold and observed many people in a stadium-like setting. They were all conversing and appeared to be somewhat excited. Off to the right there was an immensely bright light and that was the focus of activity in the auditorium. I wanted to go in desperately. As soon as I started to step over the threshold I woke up! The first thing I thought was, The Great White Throne of Judgement.

I believe Jesus was heading toward that throne of judgement. He looked as if He was heading toward a very serious matter and it was going to be something unpleasant for Him to do. I have often pondered and discussed with my family about meeting me on the hill. My parents have gone on to be with the Lord, now. I know someday, I will meet them on the hill, and I will get to spend eternity with them along with my husband. I also feel that someday I will be shown my whole life and things pertaining to my life, but this time I will remember it all.

I had this dream in 2009. It is very interesting, but I still don't have the complete understanding of parts of it. It is also quite an unusual dream. This dream is prophetic and is futuristic.

Is it Time?

I was standing amid a bunch or trees in an area where they were parted. It was at night and I saw the star lit sky. I knew I was getting ready to go up into the sky. I raised my hands above my head and placed them together like an hour hand would be. As soon as I did this I shot up into the sky and passed stars on all sides of me. I finally, abruptly, stopped in this same physical position before the sun. I knew it was the Son of God. At this time with the loudest voice I could muster I shouted, "IS IT TIME!"

The sun made a vibrating sound three times as it came closer to me as if to say, YES! The sun was huge, and It made a very loud sound as it moved closer and was very powerful.

The next scene I was before the sun at a farther distance and this time the sun had reverberated itself into four more suns and they surrounded the sun in the middle. In all, there were five suns. The other four suns were stationed at the four corners of the sun in the middle.

The next scene I am thrown back to the ground and I landed in a sitting position! It was still nighttime. I saw all the green grass and saw a huge pile of words cut up into pieces. I knew that I was to collect the words and go assemble them together, so I went and began to gather them. Then, I woke up!

I was completely astounded by this dream and I kept thinking how the Lord told me that it was time! It was time for what? I immediately knew I was to write all the words and details of the dream.

I was in the hospital and had my husband take everything home that evening because I was going home the next day. In a vision I saw my journaling notebook with a word in the corner that said, miracles. In that vision I saw the book in my side stand drawer. I distantly remember sending everything home, but I opened the drawer and there it was. This book has a huge seeing eye in the middle of the book that looks like the sun setting over the ocean. Since the dream was about the sun/Son it literally blew me away.

I immediately grabbed it and began to record the whole dream. I felt like the pile of words represented the words to the dream, but it could have been a broader meaning such as being the many words to culminate to write this book. God ALWAYS has a greater purpose. I definitely understood that the Lord was saying it was time. My questions were, is it time for the rapture? or is it time for Him to return? Why did the sun create four more replications of itself? Was something happening to the sun?

The four other suns were placed at the four corners of the sun in the dream. This caused me to pray that people would be ready for Jesus' return from the four corners of the earth. All I can say is that I know this dream was a prophetic dream from God. I have this dream depicted in a picture in my bedroom. A street artist designed it with a giant eye as the sun representing the pupil setting on the horizon of an ocean. In the center of the sun are the words "Is It Time?"

In *Lion of Judah, Is It Time?* And *Meeting on The Hill* all have a segment that emphasize that Jesus is coming soon. Each one has other aspects but conclude with that message of His coming. Be prepared for the Lord's coming! Know Him by receiving His gift of salvation. Walk in His ways and love Him with all your heart, mind and strength.

For you yourselves know perfectly that the day of the Lord so comes as a thief in the night. For when they say, "Peace and safety!" then sudden destruction comes upon them, as labor pains upon a pregnant woman. And they shall not escape. But you, brethren, are not in darkness, so that this Day should overtake you as a thief. You are all sons of light and sons of the day. We are not of the night nor of darkness. Therefore, let us not sleep, as others do, but let us watch and be sober. (1 Thes 5:2-6)

Alien Alliance

I was walking through a hotel and I stopped to chat with some people I knew. Then, I looked up and saw my family in the adjoining room. I saw my youngest brother walk in and join them. He was the last one to join the family. I then joined my family as they gathered together.

Next scene, I am walking outside the hotel down a sidewalk. It is nighttime. As I walked down the sidewalk I started looking up into the starlit sky. It was very eerie looking and downright strange looking. It did not look right and appeared a little scary. Suddenly, as I gazed at the stars they came together. As they came together, they jutted out forming a sentence. The letters were foreign, and I could not read the sentence. I knew it was a sentence because how the letters were spaced. While I was looking at these strange letters the sentence recessed back into the sky. Then again, from the stars that had gathered together, another sentence popped out in the same spot and I still could not read it. These letters and words were also very unfamiliar and did not seem to be of an earthly nature. Once again, the sentence recessed just as the other one had done. Finally, in the same place, for the third time, letters came forth from the stars. This time I could read it. It said, "Alien Alliance"

After seeing this I turned and walked further down the sidewalk. At the end of the sidewalk was a train. I boarded the train and there were a handful of people on it. The train began moving and increased its speed and began to go very erratic to the point of wrecking. The whole time I was trying, diligently, to tell the people about the "Alien Alliance". The train was driving so erratic that it was hard for them to hear me and we were being jerked around.

As I tried to tell these people about the "Alien Alliance" I saw a man out to the left of me. He was in a seat facing me and was watching me. He was sitting extremely calm and was wearing a black suit and black hat. He leans in and says to me very cunningly, "They will never believe you." "They will think you are crazy." The train abruptly comes to a halt and I wake up.

The first thing I thought to myself as I awakened was, OH, NO! America hasn't gotten into an alien alliance, have they?

As I lay in bed my mind was racing. I wondered who America had allied themselves with for the Lord to give me this dream. I knew it was not a good thing and was very troubling! I began to pray about America and this alliance they had entered into.

Being so wide awake, I got up and turned on the news checking to see if there was any confirmation to this situation. As I was watching TV my daughter woke up and walked into the room. As she was standing there at the entryway to the living room, I noticed the shirt she had on. It had a picture of a UFO on it and under it was written, We are aliens….along with a scripture from the Bible. I about fell out of my chair. You think I would be used to this by now, but God still stuns me with confirmations. I, abruptly, asked my daughter where she got that shirt! She said she had gotten the shirt from summer camp and had only worn it once. This shirt was a Christian T-shirt describing the scripture where it says we are aliens. I explained to her about the dream.

For we are aliens and pilgrims before You, As were all our fathers; Our days on earth are as a shadow, And without hope. (1 Cron. 29:15)

This was a very unusual dream with specific details. The part where my brother joined the family was meaningful because he was the last to come to the Lord in my immediate family. Like in the dream he was last to join the family. I wasn't aware of this until his funeral. A man came up and told a testimony how he had prayed with my brother weeks prior to his sudden death. I had the dream several years prior to his death, so this was an encouragement to me personally.

I knew the alien alliance had to do with America and a foreign group of people. I thought maybe they were allied with Russia or some other country for some nefarious reason. I felt strong that we were allied with some alien entity and it was highly concerning! I began to pray immediately concerning my revelation. The man in black represented Lucifer and he was trying to shut me up by saying that people would never believe me, and that people would think I was crazy. Instead of shutting me up it made me want to share this dream even more. That is a big reason why I included it in this book.

I also thought about my daughter's shirt and how it was describing the Christian as an alien. I thought that this dream could have a duo meaning of alien. It could represent the rapture where all of God's people are brought together in an alliance or union.

So, as you see, some dreams require revelation from God. Some take time to unfold their secrets, prophetically. Other dreams have aspects that are very clear with exact purpose. One thing for sure is that God communicates using dreams.

There are twenty-one dreams in the Bible. Some dreams are called night visions. Below are those who had a dream from God and where it is found in the Bible. Enjoy studying!

Dreams

1. Abimelech, Genesis 20:3
2, 3. Jacob, Genesis 28:12, 31:10
4. Laban, Genesis 31:24
5, 6. Joseph, Genesis 37:5,9
7, 8. The butler and the baker, Genesis 40:5
9, 10. Pharaoh, Genesis 41:1, 5
11. The man in Gideon's army, Judges 7:13
12. Solomon, 1 Kings 3:5
13, 14. Nebuchadnezzar, Daniel 2:3, 4:5
15. Daniel, Daniel 7:1
16, 17, 18,19. Joseph, Matthew 1:20, 2:13, 19, 22
20. The wise men, Matthew 2:12
21. Pilate's wife, Matthew 27:19

CHAPTER 17

Evidence God confirms and Encourages

"Most assuredly, I say to you, he who believes in Me, the works that I do he will do also; and greater works than these he will do, because I go to My Father. (John 14:12)

Jesus continually encouraged people in His time. He encouraged His disciples to become great in their faith. He encouraged them that they would do even greater things than Him because He would be their mediator. He has also made the believer His dwelling place. He lives in us!!! That is our promise! Possibly, Jesus meant that we would do greater things because collectively, as the body of Christ, we would and could do far beyond what He could do being one person. Then again, maybe we will see and perform many miracles that are greater than what Jesus performed. I anticipate both of these, personally.

As I have walked with Jesus these many years, I have experienced patterns. One of these patterns is how He confirms what He reveals to me or asks me to do. He sends confirmations in many different ways. He confirms to us by using other people to speak to us. He confirms by using the Word. He might confirm by coordinating a set of events that keep pointing back to the initial word or call. You might hear that still small voice inside of you that brings enlightenment. He might confirm by using a dream or a vision. He might even use a great big white billboard with words saying, "Continue Your Story" like He did with me. Every time Jesus sends a confirmation it is very encouraging and prompts us to continue staying the course.

For me, when He puts something in my mind or my heart to accomplish, He continues to send little arrows pointing to the course of direction. We need to pay attention to the signs He presents to us and not dismiss them as coincidence. If we rationalize everything away it causes us to be disobedient. I have done that, and I get mad at myself every time. I see it as a missed opportunity to fulfill God's purpose. Hopefully, I learn and grow each time. Hopefully, I find myself in disobedience less often. Here is an incident where I was disobedient. I was just too scared to step out, to speak up, and I let some tiny detail throw me off.

Many years ago, I was planning a trip to the Bahamas with my husband. I was excited about the trip and was also eagerly wondering what adventure God might set up while I was gone. So, I began praying for His will on this trip. As I sat on my bed, I saw in a vision a middle-aged woman with white hair wearing a bright red outfit. Then, the Lord zeroed me in on her shoes. They were bright red also. Then, He even gave me her name. Her name was Evelyn. The Lord told me he would put her **beside me** on the plane and that all I had to do was to tell her that He loved her and to tell her that I saw her while I was praying. Simple enough, right? Not really!

Well, I get to the airport and I am sitting with my husband waiting for our flight. All the while I'm looking for Evelyn. Suddenly, up walks a very confident woman. She has white hair. She is slender. She is wearing a red, two pieced suit and most of all she has on RED shoes. Of course, I am a bit restless and I am looking for an opportunity. I get on the plane and guess where she sits? She sits **behind me**. Now, I know this is no big deal as I look back on this whole situation, but I allowed that tiny detail to completely sidetrack me. I expected her to be beside me (next to me) not behind me. I stewed and fretted the whole flight and, sadly enough, I never spoke to this woman. I was disobedient! I should have told my husband before we left home and maybe that would have prompted me to speak to her.

To this day it grieves my heart. You know God did not need me to give her a message, yet He asked me to, and I talked myself out of it. I know somewhere along the line He got His message to her without me.

Then, maybe it was all for me to step out in faith. He had given me all the confirmation any person should need, and I still did not do what the Lord wanted me to do. I feel saddened that I allowed myself to be sidetracked by that minute detail. Of course, I will always wonder, who was this woman? What was God going to do in all this? What a witness that could have been and I will never know the answers to those questions! I believe as we are obedient to God it opens doors for Him to use us in a greater capacity. Assuredly, each time we are obedient to the Lord He receives great glory.

Here is a time that I received several confirmations, yet, this event has never happened. I believe some day it will because this set of events has earmarks of God all over it.

Surprisingly, one day I was walking through the house and I walked past my husband and said, "You know, someday I'm going to be on the 700 Club!" "I just know that someday I will!" Holy Spirit sometimes rises up within us and makes a bold statement through us and it is recognizable as such. I normally do not come off with such unrealistic statements and therefore with a grin in my heart I distinguished that it was the Lord.

A couple of weeks later, I am sitting in the teacher's lounge and a Christian teacher friend of mine walked into the lounge for lunch break. As soon as she spies me in the lounge she states loudly, "Shirley Hall, I had a dream about you last night!" "I dreamed you were on the 700 Club telling them about your books!" I just laughed and told her I felt that her dream was from God because I thought that I really was going to be on 700 Club someday. Of course, I had never mentioned that to anyone I work with, only to my husband. I also told her how I had just said that to my husband a few days ago.

A few weeks later from the time my friend had her dream I got a phone call. Guess who? It was the 700 Club. They asked me questions about my testimony, and we had a conversation about things concerning my relationship with the Lord and the books God had me write. Nothing came of that at that time, but I feel assured that someday I will be on that television show. I don't believe for a minute that all that was a coincidence. I believe God is encouraging me to know what will happen in the future. He has also confirmed what He has already, personally, revealed to me by two or three witnesses. I'm looking forward to that fulfillment of sharing my testimony and books on the 700 Club with CBN.

> *This will be the third time I am coming to you. "By the mouth of two*
> *or three witnesses every word shall be established. (2 Cor 13:1)*

Quite a few years ago I was writing my second Christian book, *Jesus, The Same Yesterday, Today and Forever,* and I struggled with completing it. I cannot tell you the number of times that God sent me word by others to finish the book. I literally had preachers on television point at me and say, "Finish that book!" Each time I recognized that the Lord was encouraging me, and I would respond, "Okay, Lord!" I finally finished the book and had it published but it was by a great amount of confirmation and encouragement from the Lord.

This next story happened many years ago but was one of the biggest surprises as I'm just sitting quietly minding my own business in a woman's meeting. He sure knows how to confirm!

I was sitting on the aisle seat in an AGLOW International meeting listening to a local pastor's wife. It was a rather large meeting of one hundred or so people. The woman was speaking about how God had called her into ministry. She was speaking with boldness and with great confidence. During her testimony I began to talk to the Lord. I started telling Him that I was never going to be able to do what this lady was doing. I was going on and on about this to the Lord when, abruptly, this woman stops dead in her speech and points to me! Loudly she proclaims, "And the Lord says, YES you will be up here like this and you are not to worry about what you will say because God will give you the words to speak!" Whoa, I literally almost fell over with shock. For one thing, why was I arguing with God about something that wasn't even happening nor was it a conceived idea of happening. It was the Holy Spirit giving me the thoughts that this was to be someday. The word from the woman was a confirmation of what I was pondering in my mind. Most often, He confirms what He calls us to. I will say, this was quite impressive, and I had no doubt to its validity. What great evidence that He is real and great evidence that He truly confirms. I love His ways! I love Him!

It was eleven years later when I started public speaking. And yes, He gave me the words to speak! I went around sharing the testimony of Hearing the voice of God. That is evidence of an amazing God that encourages and that is evidence how he confirms His word. That became a profound moment for me. I always knew I would be getting up and speaking to people long before it happened. Have you ever had a feeling God was going to use you in a particular capacity in ministry? Watch for those cues where the Holy Spirit is leading. It is sure to come to pass!

I agree that sometimes God surprises us as He plunges us into a call and sometimes, He slowly orders our footsteps into particular directions. For me, it seems like He brings lots of encouragement and confirmation. I love any way He decides to move! The funniest thing is that in college I dodged every public speaking class. Like many people, I always got nervous talking in front of others. To this day I get nervous, but once I begin to talk about the great things God has done, I get fired up and am able to speak with confidence and boldness. He has made me an overcomer in an area of insecurity!

Strangely, I have three children and all three children received Christ at the age of three and all three were baptized in the Holy Spirit at the age of three. They all spoke in tongues at the age of three. Odd huh? I thought so! Of course, I have seen my children make recommitments throughout the years, but they all had these experiences at an early age and remarkably at the same age. The only time I initiated a discussion to receive Christ was with my oldest daughter. I was divorced, and Amy and I were a family. Whatever I did she did. So, when I got saved, I asked her if she wanted to receive Jesus. She said yes and so I prayed with her. The other two children initiated their own salvation experience and their desire to be filled with the Holy Spirit.

Along with praying with Amy to receive Jesus into her heart I also prayed that she be baptized with the Holy Spirit. I saw no evidence of her being filled with the Spirit and was satisfied that she had received Christ.

And they were all filled with the Holy Spirit and began to speak with other tongues, as the Spirit gave them utterance. (Acts 2:4).

I had the most incredible experience, a few weeks later, after praying with Amy. It was the one and only time I heard the audible voice of God. I was sound asleep and in the dead of night I heard these words shouted, "Amy has the baptism of the Holy Spirit!" I jumped up and lit a candle and kept repeating the words, the Lord spoke, over and over. Why would God wake me from complete sleep to tell me this? It was so loud! He shouted it, so it must be important! I went in her bedroom and woke her up for some crazy reason. I wasn't quite sure what to do. She was three! We do silly things sometimes!

Approximately three weeks later I was filming my daughter Amy as she was sitting on my mother's lap. She had the chicken pox and could not go to daycare, so my mother was watching her. I was asking Amy some questions about staying home with grandma and was talking to her about the chicken pox when out came these funny words. She'd speak a few words, stop, and then speak some more. She was speaking in tongues. She finally began to giggle, and so did I. God had told me He baptized her in the Holy Spirit and here was some evidence of that. I have recordings of Amy's first time she spoke in tongues and I also have her singing in the Holy Spirit language at the age of four. She was so cute, and God is an Amazing God! I think this is an example of where He sends His word with signs following. (Mark 16:20) Not only did He confirm His word from that night as I slept, but it was also encouraging to know God informed me beforehand. I had prayed for her to be filled with the Holy Spirit and He thought it was important enough to shout it audibly that she was filled.

I have a very strong desire to see people saved, but I have an equally strong desire that people be filled with God's Holy Spirit. If He sent the Holy Spirit, we need the Holy Spirit! I have always been emphatic about people receiving the Holy Spirit because of the empowerment He gives. So, when I had this dream, I was not surprised. It confirmed the strong conviction within me.

> *Peter said to them, "Repent, and each of you be baptized in*
> *the name of Jesus Christ for the forgiveness of your sins; and*
> *you will receive the gift of the Holy Spirit. (Acts 2:38)*

I dreamed I was at the altar of a church and was talking to an older woman about being filled with the Holy Spirit. The next scene I am standing in the midst of a circle of people sitting in chairs. I leaned into them as I put my foot up on a chair and said, "You know, every Christian has a message, and mine is "The Baptism of the Holy Spirit" Then I woke up.

It doesn't take long after being around people to see what their heart has a passion for. God's call is the same for all, yet, He has various branches of ministry that tugs at our heart. It usually stems from where we came from in life and the experiences in that life. My daughter and son-in-law have a strong call to minister to those with addictions because of where they came from. What tugs at your heart?

You will see a strong thread through my writing concerning the Holy Spirit and that is because of my background, my experiences, my mother and because of the Word. It is important that we live an empowered Christian Life. We must have a powerful witness for the world to see. Our life should exude that persona. Our light must shine brightly for all to see. Receive the baptism of the Holy Spirit! Allow the Holy Spirit to empower you, help you, teach you, gift you, and make you more like Christ.

"If you love Me, [b]keep My commandments. And I will pray the Father, and He will give you another [c]Helper, that He may abide with you forever— (John14:15-16)

CHAPTER 18

Evidence God Heals

Then He said to the man, "Stretch out your hand." And he stretched it out, and it was restored as whole as the other.

Then the Pharisees went out and plotted against Him, how they might destroy Him. But when Jesus knew it, He withdrew from there. And great multitudes followed Him, and He healed them all. (Matt 12:13-15)

Healing was a major part of Jesus' ministry and in some cases, He healed everyone as it is stated in this verse. I want to see where people are healed to this magnitude. I have prayed and pressed God many years to understand why healing is not this prevalent.

Healing comes in many forms and can be physical, mental, emotional or spiritual. I received salvation at age 24 because a girl I worked with told me her mother was healed through watching and praying with people on the 700 Club. I have also seen people restored back to the Father once healing occurred concerning their past. My pastor prayed for another pastor from a local church and he was miraculously healed from cancer. I have seen and heard evidence that God heals. This chapter will focus on physical healing.

I, myself, experienced healing when I first became a Christian. I don't talk about it a whole lot because of the nature of the healing. When I was in my twenties I was diagnosed with cists throughout my breast and it was very painful. On a Friday night I went to a church in a neighboring town. As I was standing in a healing line the woman began to pray for me. She did not ask me why I was seeking prayer, but the Holy Spirit gave her wisdom. She was exact in her discernment of my need for healing and she began praying for two areas of my body. Once she prayed, I had extreme heat within my breast. I remember feeling the heat even as I left the meeting. It was quite incredible. From that night forward I was completely healed from the cysts. They were completely gone and have never returned.

The other area this woman prayed for that night was for my abdomen. I had been diagnosed with a spastic colon while living in California. It was very painful as well, but I was not healed that night. Shortly thereafter, my mother prayed for my healing as she prayed for me to be baptized in the Holy Spirit. I cannot tell the exact moment when I was healed, but the problem disappeared. I had issues for several years, so I was tremendously grateful when God healed me.

My husband said, when he was a little boy, he prayed for his blind dog and he was healed of blindness. That is remarkable! My husband has always told me an incredible story about his uncle from when he was a young boy. His great uncle Alvy was struck with some strange, unknown disease. When his family went to visit him, my husband witnessed family continuously wiping him down from oily oozing sores. His uncle could not wear much clothing because the problem was so extreme and whatever was oozing from his body would ruin his clothes. His grandparents were Christians and believed in healing. Alvy was not a believer and was awfully sick. So, one day the family called an ambulance and had Alvy taken to Louisville, Kentucky for a healing service. Miraculously, Alvy was completely healed from this debilitating malady. He received Jesus as his Lord and savior after his healing. I'd say healing made him a believer!

God definitely heals!

My grandmother had bone cancer and after men from church came and prayed for her the bone cancer was gone. She had it verified from her doctor that she no longer had bone cancer in her shoulder. I have read many testimony books that tell about miraculous healing and have also seen many testimonies from various media outlets.

Even though there is evidence of healing all around the world it seems that I'm not seeing it as much as how the Bible describes it. I desire that all be healed in my family, in my church, and in my community! I have questioned God about healing because it should be occurring more frequently. I pray for people to be healed but rarely see it manifest. I feel like I have all the faith needed, but maybe I lack faith. I hear about healing in the United States and throughout the world, but I want to see it right here in my midst! I want to experience it just like Jesus and the disciples did! I have prayed for the gift of miracles for healing to transpire. I am very drawn to people with disabilities and pray quietly as I walk by them in public. At times, with permission, I just lay my hands on them and pray for healing. I pray for people quite often, such as friends and family members and do not see people being healed. My son has multiple sclerosis and I want to see him healed!

Assuredly, I see every aspect of the Bible being manifested, but healing seems to be stalled. I expect healing to be widespread! That is what I believe, and I feel frustrated. I want it and I always anticipate it for others and for myself. I have suffered with several maladies for many years of my life. The worst physical issue I have is muscular pain. I have had muscular pain for over thirty years. My muscles are not normal. My larger muscles are lumpy and appear to be fragmented and it causes lots of pain. The only answer I ever got from a doctor is that it is fibromyalgia which simply means chronic pain.

My greatest frustration is seeing people sick. Oftentimes, when there is an alter call for healing the whole alter is packed. It is heartbreaking! One time I was at a church and most of the church was at the alter to receive healing. That should not be happening! I am on a quest to continue pressing God for healing. I am ready for a Healing Breakthrough!

I have prayed many different scriptures for healing for my body and for others. I have spoken blessings over and over for every part of my body. I have broken generational curses and have engaged in spiritual warfare over my body. I have stayed in repentance and have always stayed in a state of forgiveness. I do not believe God wants me sick either. His word is contrary to that belief. I have felt victory in every part of my life except with these physical issues. I remain cheerful and happy and have the peace of God, yet I remain in constant pain. Unfortunately, I do not have an answer. I am waiting for some type of revelation concerning my condition. I know one thing, I will never quit, never slow down, nor will I ever get bitter over having these physical issues. I am pressing toward the mark of the prize of that high calling and I am determined to pray more, care more, and love more no matter what condition I am in. I will continue to pray for the sick and help those in need as long as I am able because the Lord has done great things for me!

> *"Heal the sick, cleanse the lepers, raise the dead, cast out demons. Freely you have received, freely give. (Matthew 10:8)*

> *And when He had called His twelve disciples to Him, He gave them power over unclean spirits, to cast them out, and to heal all kinds of sickness and all kinds of disease. (Matthew 10:1)*

Are there any frustrations in your life? Is there an area where you struggle and cannot seem to get the victory? You are certainly not alone! All you have to do is look around and see where the power of Christ is needed. Some people have waited a lifetime to see family members get saved. Others may still be waiting to see a spouse delivered from alcohol. There is tremendous amount of suffering throughout the world and as we continue to believe and trust God, He will provide what we need. Love others going through trials and tribulations and they will love us through ours. Imagine Jesus on the cross and how He must have felt through the crucifixion.

CHAPTER 19

Evidence That God Answers Prayer

Now this is the confidence that we have in Him, that if we ask anything according to His will, He hears us.

And if we know that He hears us, whatever we ask, we know that we have the petitions that we have asked of Him. (1 John 5:14-15)

Early on, I began to see evidence of a God that answered prayers. The very first prayer I had answered had to do with smoking cigarettes. I had smoked for nine years and when I gave my life to the Lord I really wanted to quit. Although, I had made many attempts to quit over the years and was never successful. I had heard that some people received instant deliverance from smoking and that is what I was praying. I had been praying for several weeks that God would deliver me from the desire to smoke. I knew that if I got delivered it would have to be God. Realistically, I knew many people had quit smoking on their own, so I knew it was not impossible. Both my parents quit smoking years earlier, but I had really made some attempts and was not able to shake the desire. I was smoking 2 packs a day and I really loved it, but I hated it too. It seemed to make me sick. I would get terrible coughs and my throat seemed to get infected easily. I just did not want to smoke any more. I felt that it was a terrible witness and I was ready to believe God for a miracle.

After praying for several weeks, I was driving home from work one night. I worked at the Marriott Inn and worked a night shift in the dining room whereas, I normally worked day shift. I was out of cigarettes and would normally stop at the gas station right by my house, but this night was different. On the way home I said to myself that I was not going to stop at the gas station to get cigarettes. My next thought was that I did not think I was ever going to smoke again. Yeah right….wonder where that came from? Yep, it was the Holy Spirit and from that night on I never had another cigarette. I never wanted one and I had absolutely no withdrawal from the nicotine. It was a miracle that I desperately wanted and needed! What a miracle! I was so pumped when that prayer was answered. My faith was in the cloud level. I did not have one single withdrawal after smoking nine years. I used to have withdrawals after five minutes, after I ate, after I took a shower, after I got out of bed, after, after after! So, to absolutely not have even one desire to smoke and to not have even one teeny tiny withdrawal, I had to tell everyone. That was all the evidence I needed, but thankfully, there was much more evidence of God's answers to prayer to come!

God has an endless supply of miracles and endless ways of doing them. One scripture states that we need to ask Him for things and that we do not have because we have not asked Him for it. (James 4:2b)

The next prayer that God answered was for a bed. I had been living in housing after my divorce and I did not even have beds for me or my daughter. We lived in government housing and all we had were mattresses thrown on the floor. It did not bother me before I was a Christian, but it did afterward. I did not have anything back in those days even with working every day. I certainly noticed some changes in my thinking after becoming a Christian.

I had been praying for God to give me a bed. At this point, I was believing Him for anything, and I needed a bed. People told me about the faith of a mustard seed, and I believed He could do anything. One morning before going to work I walked to the dumpster to throw something away. Lo and behold, there was a complete bed leaning against the concrete wall. It had the headboard, footboard, and the rails and it was the exact same size as my mattress. I scooped it up and praised Jesus all the way back to my apartment. I had some royal blue paint, so I painted it and my daughter used that bed for many years. I was so excited that God answered my prayer and gave me a bed.

I had become a Christian when I was 24 and was already divorced and had a sweet little girl. I had started back to college and was very busy getting back on track. I had a very strong desire to get married again and do things right this time around. During that time, I had all kinds of people tell me that I needed to go out and that that was the only way I was going to find a husband. I would always tell them that God would bring me a husband! They would just laugh and repeat that I needed to get out there. I was too busy… To Get Out There!

Of course, during that time I prayed for God to bring me a husband and I began praying everything for that man that God was going to bring me. I prayed for my future husband's life and prayed for certain qualities. After two years, a very close friend told me about some guy she went to church with and I promptly told her to fix me up with him. We had never moved in on someone so unsuspecting, so quickly.

In a few weeks, after our first blind date, Larry and I fell in love and were married in eight months. We have been married for 32 years and are still in love. God answers prayer as we wait on His perfect timing.

I have a strong governmental call on my life. I spend a fair amount of time praying for the nation and for the government. I am especially praying for the President of the United States. For years, I prayed for the body of Christ as the Lord focused me on areas of need. In my early days, I prayed for people I worked with or people that just happened to be walking down the street. I had a real burden to pray for those kids I had gone to high school with! I cried and prayed for hours for my best friend from high school and for many others. I prayed for them to get saved and to know the Lord. Around three years later my best friend called me and told me about getting saved while she was in a business meeting. She heard the Lord speak to her. A few years after receiving Christ, she called me crying and said the Lord showed her that I had prayed for her and that was how she came to know Him. She even thanked me which made me think the Lord really did reveal that to her. I was excited to get a confirmation that praying for her brought her to the Lord. For her to say that to me with such emotion I really feel it was evidence that He answered my specific prayer for her. What a blessing to have a part in my best friend's getting to know the same God that I loved so much. Are there specific people where God gives you a heart to pray?

I had a two-year stint where I had this real burden for my uncle and his son. I prayed on the way to work during these two years and prayed they would get saved. My uncle did not believe in God and my cousin did not seem to think much of God either. My heart really hurt for them and it was noticeable that the Holy Spirit was having me pray for them. Eventually, they both received Christ into their lives. I will never forget when I got the call on Christmas day. My aunt called me and said, "Guess what?" I said, "What?" She said, "Well, think of the best news you could hear!" I said, "Uncle Dave got saved?" She said yes and began to tell me what happened. God answers prayer! As you are diligent to pray for those heavy upon your heart, you will see the faithfulness of God.

Just a few weeks ago, I prayed that God would give my brother's girlfriend a dream because she told me that she just did not believe the whole thing about Jesus. I had been talking to her about receiving Jesus and then I asked her why it was so hard for her to make that confession. She simply stated, "I just don't believe it!" I was very shocked at what she said. Honestly, I didn't realize she felt that way. So, I felt like if God gave her a dream she would believe. It was no more than three weeks and we had plans to run around and do errands. The first thing she tells me when she got in the car was that she had a very strange dream and wanted to know what I thought. She began to tell me that she dreamed that she died, and all these other people died too. She said they were all in this one place getting ready to go to heaven. They were all getting to go to heaven, and they told her she could not go. She said she was extremely sad. At that time, I did not divulge that I had prayed for The Lord to give her a dream, but I did tell her I felt that it was a dream from God. I just made some kind of statement to her that she knew how to make that right. And I said, "You have to go to heaven!" Being around my family she has heard many times what to do to receive Christ. I love her so much and I want her to know how much God cares for her.

I pray that God will give people dreams so that Jesus can reveal Himself to them. I can't recall praying for someone I knew, like that, to have a dream. Holy Spirit must have led me to pray that because the answer came very quickly. As we seek God, the Holy Spirit will give us specifics to pray. Have you ever had a random thought to pray for someone? When specific thoughts come to pray about someone or something, oftentimes, it is a prompting from the Holy Spirit.

Years ago, I walked by the television and there was a man and a woman talking. I paused and listened, and this woman was telling how her brother had been a prisoner of war for seven years. Surprisingly, I began to cry and weep over her brother. I had not had that happen out of the blue like that before, so I listened closer to the situation. I had never heard of Terry Anderson before that day. Terry was an American journalist that was taken hostage for nearly seven years by a group of Hezbollah in Beirut Lebanon. He was the Middle East bureau chief of the Associated Press. They threw him in a trunk of a vehicle and imprisoned him.

One week, after the incident where I interceded for him, Terry Anderson was released with a couple of other men that had been imprisoned with him. That was in 1991. I could not believe my eyes as I saw this unfold on the news. Was my prayer the only prayer that enabled his release? I would say not! In fact, there were probably many sources orchestrated by God for his release. Although, God answered my prayer and I felt grateful to be a part of that. Equally as exciting, is that the Lord allowed me to see the answer to my prayer! It is important to continue to pray even when it does not make sense or even when we do not understand.

On Tuesday nights I had prayer with several people from church. This one night while we were all praying, something rose up in me. These words came up and out, "I pray for the Jericho walls to come down!" I kept saying this several times consecutively and found the words odd. Three days later I was watching the news and the reporter began to tell about a standoff in Jericho over in the middle east. They were showing pictures of the scene of some compound being under siege. He said there had been a battle throughout the day with severe fighting around this compound. He told how they had finally won the battle and routed out the terrorists. The next words the reporter said blew me away! He exclaimed, "Today, the walls of Jericho came down!" I began cheering for the answered prayer and felt privileged to see it play out on national television.

Many years ago, I used to pray something which seemed somewhat bizarre. I prayed non-stop about women and people being captured. I live in America! And this seemed a bit over the top. I was not aware of slavery or people being imprisoned against their will in our nation. I always thought about that in other countries, but I felt like it was for our country. I prayed that for at least four years. I kept envisioning mostly women and children being captured. I prayed that God would give them wisdom to get out of their situation and for them to get rescued. I seemed to go on and on concerning this, but I did not really understand it. One day, I glanced at a newspaper and there was a picture showing this window at the top of a huge empty warehouse. The headlines stated that these two children, a little boy and girl, were rescued from being held captive by banging on the window. People walking by on the street below heard them banging on the window and they were then rescued.

I am not saying they were rescued because of me; I just think God wanted me to see that this kind of thing was happening. That newspaper article confirmed to me that the prayer for captured people was needed and so, I continued to pray even more concerning this kind of thing.

Fifteen years later…

Now, I completely understand why I prayed in that manner because of what I have been finding out. I have been reading and studying about human trafficking here in the United States and around the world. When I first heard about this, I could not believe what I was hearing. The details were so horrifying that I literally cried for three months concerning child trafficking. I have now been investigating this for almost two years. No wonder the Lord had me praying about people being captured. Trafficking rings are throughout the U.S. and worldwide. Two thousand children are missing each day in America according to the national statistics. That is astounding! People are just now waking up to this situation and many people are being arrested for human trafficking. Thankfully, I am seeing God answer these prayers. I am fervently praying and asking God to rescue these people. Please pray for these trafficking rings to be destroyed and for the people to be rescued. Children are the largest group of victims. Pedophilia and occultic practices are destroying these children's lives along with their families.

*Rejoice always, pray without ceasing, in everything give thanks; for this
is the will of God in Christ Jesus for you. Do not quench the Spirit.
Do not despise prophecies. Test all things; hold fast what is good.
(1 Thes 5:14-21)*

Since I became aware of the human trafficking, I began a prayer group
at my church. We started to stand in the gap for those that were helpless
through trafficking and began praying for the upcoming presidential
election. My church allowed me to have a couple of community prayer
dates and even had a couple of connect groups solely for prayer. Then
God began showing and exposing many atrocities going on in America.
There were crimes being committed against humanity! The Lord gave me
the scripture where Ezekiel is shown atrocities and let me know He was
exposing what was happening in our own country. Just like the scripture
below, God began taking me deeper and deeper into the corruption in the
United States of America.

*Furthermore, He said to me, "Son of man, do you see what they are
doing, the great abominations that the house of Israel commits here,
to make Me go far away from My sanctuary? Now turn again, you
will see greater abominations." So, He brought me to the door of the
court; and when I looked, there was a hole in the wall. Then He said
to me, "Son of man, dig into the wall"; and when I dug into the wall,
there was a door. And He said to me, "Go in, and see the wicked
abominations which they are doing there." So, I went in and saw,
and there—every sort of creeping thing, abominable beasts, and all
the idols of the house of Israel, portrayed all around on the walls.*

One thing led to another and at this time I have joined in with two
teams of intercessors a week. Severe corruption seemed to be taking over
in some of the highest offices in America and the Holy Spirit showed
me this root of corruption. I knew this root had to be dug up and every
part of the root needed to be removed. These are the specifics God has
had me praying. I, along with several other women have been praying for
our country and praying for our president. We have not let up for three
years! Many Christian men and women woke up around our nation as

God began exposing the grave darkness. They began stepping up their intercession for our nation. God has heard our prayers and is answering these prayers concerning our nation.

One of the greatest answers to prayer has just broken through! As a sinister group plotted to overthrow a duly elected president here in America a huge cover up began in our nation. It is now being exposed and major investigations are beginning. Hopefully, Indictments are coming forth soon. Acts of treason have been exposed. A socialist/communistic thread has also been exposed. We are still praying for that to be brought down. The mainstream media has also been involved in the coverup. Instead of backing off as they have been exposed, they have doubled down with their propaganda, making many people totally unaware of what has been going on.

So, I rejoice for God called a large group of His people to pray for a dire situation and now He is bringing forth the fruit of our labor.

Praise God!!!! For He cares for us!

If My people who are called by my name, will humble themselves and pray, and seek my face, and turn from their wicked ways, then I will hear from heaven, and forgive their sin and heal their land. (2Chron 7:14)

CHAPTER 20

Evidence God Imparts Wisdom

For the Lord gives wisdom; From His mouth come knowledge and understanding; He stores up sound wisdom for the upright; He is a shield to those who walk uprightly; He guards the paths of justice and preserves the way of His saints. (Prov. 2:6-8)

As I read the Bible, I hear great wisdom from Genesis to Revelation. God has communicated wonderful messages to us in unique fashion. While reading the Bible, I feel moved and enlightened. It is such a beacon of light. God's words are life and they produce sustenance to the reader. There is an anointing on God's word, and it has transforming power for positive change. His word is a light unto our path and a lamp unto our feet as stated in Ps. 119:105. Not only is the Word captivating because of what it says, but because of how it is written.

Only God could create all the styles of writing that are used in the old and new testaments of the Bible. There are letters, poetry, parables, and prophecy. It is incredible how scripture from the old testament describes future events and a coming Messiah. It is a wonderful historical document containing valuable genealogical records and is full of types and shadows. It is a complete multi-dimensional document that is classed as the number one selling book of all time!

The Holy Spirit inspired writers to record God's word from Genesis to revelation. The Holy Spirit came upon those in the old testament to bring the written and spoken word. Whereas, in the new testament people were indwelled with the Holy Spirit being inspired from within.

As Jesus walked on this earth, He amazed people by what He said and how He said it. His teaching style was incredibly engaging. His wisdom astounded His audience as He used parables, object lessons, comparisons and dialogue. He used questioning to involve His listeners and He used concrete objects to get His point across.

I too have been amazed at the words I have heard as I journaled. It seems that Jesus could minister to one person or two thousand and be happy in either situation. At times, He is humorous in what He says and throws people off guard continually by His wisdom. I have learned so much over the past thirty-four years by listening to Him, by way of His Spirit. I have immensely enjoyed this two-way relationship. If I never heard His voice again, I think I would die of a broken heart. That is what His Words have meant to me. I experienced Jesus' teaching styles as He taught me to hear His voice. Now that I have all that He taught me recorded in journals I can recognize the Lords varying styles. He often asked me questions, used metaphors, and used puns to bring in humor as I sat before Him. Jesus used many styles while teaching great audiences which are depicted in the new testament. That is why people followed Him around. They could not get enough of His wisdom! People were drawn in by His varying styles of teaching. And, of course, the miracles were the signs that followed Him which amazed many. As Jesus carried the anointing to communicate, He was able to capture the hearts of His listeners and deposit truth.

Throughout my times with the Lord He has given me little tidbits of wisdom. They are proverbial in style and I love them. I am in no way comparing what I hear to scripture! I have just recognized that what I'm hearing is characteristic to the way the Lord speaks. The words Jesus has spoken to me show me evidence of a wise God that cares enough to impart a facet of Himself to His creation.

Sometimes, I do not completely understand all the things I hear, and I am okay with that. I have understood enough to know that Jesus is who He says He is, and I have understood enough that I know He is going to do what He says He is going to do. I have known only a loving, peaceful God that seems to have a desire for us to know Him in a very personal way. Much revelation has come in hindsight as I began to study God's word and began to see similarities. I am just telling a story of what happened as Jesus began to teach me to hear His voice.

Every ounce of the Bible is divinely inspired by the Holy Spirit and is backed by God Almighty. We won't ever figure out everything, but I certainly think there is so much more to discover about the Lord, His word, and His kingdom. The more I learn the more questions I have. The more I experience demonstrates that there are greater things to encounter in this relationship with Him.

In this chapter I am going to share many of the words of wisdom Jesus spoke to me during my journaling time. Again, everything I share is exactly how I heard them while praying in the Spirit. I do not change any words but copy them directly from my journals. Some of these are thought provoking and some are being used as comparisons. I hope you enjoy hearing these sayings just as I have.

> *Now we have received, not the spirit of the world, but the Spirit who is from God, that we might know the things that have been freely given to us by God. These things we also speak, not in words which man's wisdom teaches but which the Holy Spirit teaches, comparing spiritual things with spiritual. (1 Cor.2:12-13)*

As you read these simple tidbits of wisdom you might want to circle the ones that are meaningful to you. There may be several that speak to you personally.

1. Be at peace for the ways I teach have remained the same. No man recalls his teacher unless he taught him something.
2. I scan this earth looking for the one, the two, the many I may send that I may send one, two and or many to do my will.
3. Make a way for truth so that truth may make a way.
4. Climb a hill. Climb a mountain. Both are feats for the body. Both are challenges. So, therefore, one can acclaim victory as one conquers its task.

5. Take a grain of wheat, just one. Look at its possibility. It can be crushed to produce. Add it to many other grains and the possibilities are endless.

6. Treat others with respect so as to be one of credibility. Be known as one who is credible and respectable.

7. Care for the old for their ways are old. An old way is an old way. But an old man cares for the way of old.

8. Each step man takes is a step in a particular direction, but, when a step is misplaced complacency sets in.

9. It's a gift of God that gives all the ideas that race throughout this earth. Why should a man say it is mine when all is the Lords?

10. Ears do hear but hearts don't receive. Mouths do speak but actions are weak.

11. Truth is present, and truth is given. Receive the truth to have and possess full enlightenment.

12. So where shall a man lie? Shall he be in the realm of maximized works or shall he dwell in lethargy? Take a pint of anything. Take a quart of anything. Which would you choose? The larger amount is desirable. Go for the maximum. Go for the most of all things. Teach others the same thing.

13. A truth is truth. Stand on it. Walk on it. Show it off. Share it. Bring it wherever you go. Give it away.

14. Take my word and bend it into every outlet so that it may go out with power. Take it always with you.

15. Abide by my truth alone for it is truth that will set many free. It has been released to reveal the false. As truth stands beside false, false has to bow. Only as truth stands alongside false will it bow. If false stands alone, it stands until it is revealed.

16. Speak the plain truth. Truth is very exact and is alone truth. It needs nothing else to surround it or crowd it. Truth is simple in nature and is above and below a surface of all things. In an event where truth is not presented the surface is tainted and all that is within is tainted also. That which is seen and that which is unseen is corrupted.

17. There is power in surrender. You forfeit all, yet, you gain all that is on the other side.

18. It is man alone that lies in a kingdom, all his own, for he creates it, dwells in it and falls before it.

19. Give ear to my words that the days may be full and rich and full of my glory. Take each day and dissect it. Which part will carry on and which will go by the wayside? Distinguish between the two and separate yourself from that which is eternal and that which is temporary. (look at them) Cling to the eternal.

20. Space has been given you. Place has been prepared for you and pace has been designed for you. Now, all three are perfect for you. (Place, space and pace) How good it is for you this day. Peace be still.

21. Deliberate among yourselves to deliberately use the word of God. It will be the train you ride among many sports cars. None can beat it. None can out power it. It goes according to its course and it stays on course. All else stands back to allow it to run its course. Whole towns are split by it. The course of my word continues throughout time, just as a train. Its purpose is to <u>carry</u> out the plan of God perfecting the way of the saints.

22. Mountains and valleys are alike in one thing. They both slope one way or another. They are reflective of one another. It takes a strong man to climb a mountain. But it takes a strong man to climb up out of a valley. To come off of a mountain is like a trip to the valley. It is easy to come down. So, the ways the man can go are many yet, are the same.

23. Respond slowly yet respond timely.

24. A man is appointed to die only once. But a man who continues to die daily is worthy of his hire.

25. Count your many blessings for they shall increase into great abundance. The foolish shall not receive such an abundance.

26. Relentlessly, time is giving over to the kingdom with the power thrust of the Lord God Almighty. It has no choice!

27. Knowledge can beat the best of men. Although man thinks he masters knowledge! He is yet to come into the knowledge of God.

28. Be at a place and settle in. Be at a place and busy about. Be at a pace and absolutely be still. See, the three of these will make a man

completely fulfilled in his place of occupation for there is a time for all things in all places.

29. Selfish pride is one that looks at itself in the mirror and says, "Look what I have done and look what I have!" Love looks in the mirror and says, "Look what the Lord has done and look what I have become!"

30. Hesitate only to disregard the trivial. But, ponder on many ideas that will bring forth a great garden of pleasures.

31. Flee seven directions and come back unprepared. Stay in one spot and receive discipline.

32. There will be a day that kingdoms will rise, and kingdoms will fall and yet, my kingdom has not fallen nor, has it risen. For there is no kingdom of mine, that is not, and then is, and is, then is not.

33. He who stands under a fallen rock gets crushed. He who dances in my presence gets fullness of joy.

34. My hand is secure, and your grip must be secure. Take not security in the things of this world.

35. My ways are frequented by many. But many frequently miss my ways.

36. An appetite is strongest when one has worked all day and comes into rest. But my kingdom is just the opposite. When one hungers he will become a worker. As he hungers, he is filled, and then it gives him stamina to go out.

37. If a man avails much on his own, then in his mind he needs no God. But if a man has seen the plan of God in his life then he will relinquish his life unto me.

38. Diligently, delight in my kingdom. See its ways and see its countenance. It is arrayed with beauty and it is full of courtships.

39. Take lies and turn them around to be truth for within a lie there lies truth.

40. Reach out your hand. What do you see? You see nothing. When I reach out my hand what do you see? You see where a sacrifice was made. Something has been removed because it was a sacrifice. Whenever sacrifice comes something must go.

41. Ponder on this! Take a piece of bacon and fry it. It reduces in size. Now take the flesh and crucify it and it reduces in size. The heat does the same for both.

42. Tidily winks! Take one to move another. This is how I do with my people.

43. Delight in my ways. Take a child for instance. You take him to the fair and he wants more. You take him to the zoo, and he wants more, but take him in your arms and see his content.

44. The birds have the sky to fly. The animals roam the earth, but man shall soar by the Spirit of God.

45. A worn-out old shoe can be a good thing for it is an outward appearance of something that needs repair. But, with a clock, a brokenness that lies within is not easily detected.

46. As one with wisdom of God and one with the wisdom of the Word, there can be no mistake of any matter of truth.

47. The wise would take every opportunity to listen to me for one hour and then go on to the second hour.

48. The light has come and so has the day begun.

49. The hand that carries the money needs to take care of the hand that takes charge of the home. And likewise, the hand that takes care of the home needs to take care of the hand with the money.

50. Tall trees truly do stand tall, but, does a short stump reap the benefit of what it used to be? I say not! So, don't be a short stump. Be a tall tree.

51. A suitcase can be empty or full. When it's full you are going someplace. When it's empty it's stored away. I desire that your suitcase be full; to be ready to go. Read the Word!

52. Speak truth and walk in truth. Don't make up your own truths for your truths are not my truths. Your truths are twisted. They are like unto a pretzel. They are self-serving. They come back to self.

53. There is a peach. It falls from the tree and knows from where it comes. Yet, the apple that is thrown under the peach tree is confused. For the apple does not belong to the peach tree. So, I say, that when a man comes unto me, he knows the way. But if he doesn't come unto me, he shall not know of his way.

54. Find a great teacher and you will find a student that is yearning to learn. You, eventually, will find a person that is well knowledgeable of the things taught. If the person applies what he has learned, he will perfect the knowledge learned. He then walks in the knowledge.

55. Take this can of soda and shake it. From the outside you cannot tell that it has incurred a shaking. No signs are available. But as soon as you open it, there it goes all over the place. Then there is sure evidence of the shaking. This is like a man that has been upset over a matter and then keeps it to himself.

56. There is no sign to see when a man is angered and holds onto his tongue. But when a man is angered and does not hold onto his tongue then it is like a ship that crashes into the shore and becomes shipwrecked. He then cannot pull back and work his way out because by his words he is trapped. Do you see?

57. A man spends a lifetime in truth, or he spends a lifetime trying to survive.

58. Take a choice given to you and choose wisely. For it is in the choosing that will warrant the success of a thing.

59. Upholding truth makes a man merry in his heart over many matters. Teach others the truths that I bestow. They need to hear the miracles of God and not a few steps of success.

60. Take patience and turn it around and it creates irritation. Take patience and use it and it will bring peace of mind.

61. An ounce of willingness is worth a pound of effort.

62. The backside of every dish is known of its maker. So, shall the Earth be turned and be known of its maker.

63. Suffer not the little children. Do not deprive, those lacking in depth of knowledge of the Lord, for the sake of their lack.

64. Speak truth always and know that the truth is the only way that lies will die. The death of a lie is a good day!

65. A day of destruction comes nigh to the dwelling of the one who believes lies and embraces them.

66. Dreams are likely to happen if a man delights in making them happen. A man with no dream shall surely die and wither up. But a man that carries a dream within his heart has a prize worth

presenting. A man that counts on fulfilling his dream shall be rewarded. For it is I that has placed the dream within, and no man has not a dream. But the man that carries out his dream is truly doing unto me, that which I have given unto him.

My hopes are that you will be encouraged to seek out this God of wisdom. He has so much for each of us! He has such great plans for us to prosper and will give us what we need to accomplish great things in His name! As we value His words, hopefully we will record them. I have had a lifetime to record His words to me and now He is having me share them in this book. I want people to know that…

He is a GREAT GOD with GREAT WISDOM!

If any of you lacks wisdom, let him ask of God, who gives to all liberally and without reproach, and it will be given to him. (James 1:5)

CHAPTER 21

Evidence God Helps
Us to Overcome

*"And they overcame him because of the blood of the Lamb
and because of the word of their testimony, and they did not
love their life even when faced with death.* (Rev. 12:11)

To overcome is the ability to succeed or do well during a difficulty. Life is
full of struggles and God will always give us whatever we need to overcome
during these adversities. Jesus shed His blood on the cross giving us the
power to overcome. As we receive His precious sacrifice of the work on the
cross, we will begin to have testimonies showing evidence of our success.
The Christian is made more than a conqueror and the position of defeat is
not for us, but for our enemy.

Half of our battle is against our own flesh or against fleshly actions
of others. The other half of our battle is with the enemy. Our enemy is
God's enemy trying to kill, steal and destroy anything belonging to God.
Since we belong to God there is a great battle over us and against us. We
overcome when we apply God's Word to our situations and when we walk
in the authority Jesus bestowed upon us. We are joint heirs with Jesus and
being joint heirs allows us to walk in the same privileges as Him. Although,
we would not be able to accomplish the will of the Father without the
Holy Spirit. The real issue for believers is that we are not using all that has
been given, and that includes me! We need to realize we are filled with the

same power as Christ and therefore acknowledge that power by activating whatever is needed for each situation. Holy Spirit will comfort us, impart wisdom, or show us a way out of these difficulties in our life. Since the Holy Spirit dwells within us He is literally going through every adversity we endure. If we yield to Him, listen to His leadings, He will help us overcome through these difficult times.

As I look back on my life there are many encounters with God that surely helped me to overcome during times of struggle. There were times when I would get caught up in the turmoil of my difficulty and God had to remind me that I was a born-again, Holy Spirit empowered believer. Out of those times I accumulated great testimonies where I overcame!

I am a retired teacher now, but there were many years of hardship during my teaching career. I enjoyed the creative part of teaching and I treasured the children. I taught in a west-end school for twenty-four years and I loved it, but it was a very challenging job. If it had not been for the Lord, I probably would have quit and not finished to enjoy these days of retirement. He helped me through the more challenging years with coping methods and encouragement. Those that teach understand completely!

One year I struggled so much because of poor classroom behaviors that I often found myself in tears and crying before the Lord. It was Christmas break and I was dreading to return to school. I was on the floor of my living room crying my eyes out over the current school year. I was telling the Lord how horrible it was and asking for help. Unexpectedly, I saw in a vision a gigantic bone with pieces of meat hanging from it and these vicious vultures were picking meat off the bone. I cried even louder and yelled out to the Lord, "See what they are doing to me?" "They are picking me apart!" Immediately I heard a response from the Lord, "But, *LOOK* at how the flesh is disappearing!"

**Oh my! I rolled over onto my back and
immediately broke into laughter!**

When I finished laughing, I exclaimed in response back to
God, "Lord, if you're getting rid of the flesh, okay!"

I could not believe it! When the Lord put it in that context, I completely understood that through that process He was allowing the flesh to disappear from me. I really was amazed and very much relieved. I was even downright happy about it! I went back to school with a completely different attitude and I did not seem to struggle as severely from that point forward. If God was truly doing a work in me through that struggle I was satisfied. I welcomed Him to mold me and shape me even when it was painful. Thankfully, God encouraged me during one of the roughest years of teaching. He enabled me to stay in His will by showing me the good that He was bringing out of that difficult situation. I was grateful that He showed me what He was doing in the process.

So then, those who are in the flesh cannot please God. (Ro 8:8)

Another time I was praying, and in a vision, I saw this enormous red bricked wall. I heard the Lord telling me to come up the wall. I looked at the wall and could not see any way to get up the wall and so I said, "I can't!" He then responded, "Yes, you can!" As soon as He said this to me, I began seeing myself climbing that wall with amazing skills. Suddenly, bricks started protruding everywhere as if to stop me. As each one protruded, I grabbed it and threw it down crashing to the ground. The Lord then spoke, "I will put the enemy beneath your feet!" In the vision, I continued and successfully got up to the top of that wall. That was a strange, yet memorable vision and I never forgot it. I found it encouraging as I used it to pray, but not as encouraging as when I got the complete understanding what this wall symbolized.

A few years later after receiving this vision, I was walking from the parking lot into school as I had every day. I felt dread! I did not want to go to work because it had become so hard. The demands were difficult to meet, and the students were quite unruly. It became such a daily battle! I knew it was going to be another hard day's work! As I walked up the sidewalk to the school entrance I looked over and up. One side of the building was nothing but red brick and reached the height of approximately three stories. It was the side where the gym was located. I was elated at the revelation! This was that **red brick wall** which was symbolized in my vision. This was God's call on my life. He called me to this place, and He was going to give me the strength and the abilities to overcome in this climb. Not only that, but He was going to put the enemy beneath my feet. What an encouragement from the Lord!

In my final three years of teaching I walked from the parking lot into school each day and I looked up at that massive **red brick wall** and remembered the promise of the Lord. I knew I could make it with His help. Those final three years were very difficult, but the Lord gave me His word and a vision to help me through them. What a difference it made! That was tangible evidence from God providing a way to overcome. He certainly caused me to be triumphant in that situation!

> Look for God in your struggles! Seek Him, for He is surely there to be found encouraging you all the way!

> *No temptation has overtaken you except such as is common to man; but God is faithful, who will not allow you to be tempted beyond what you are able, but with the temptation will also make the way of escape, that you may be able to bear it. (1 Cor. 10:13)*

God's word helps me to overcome situations that seem too big for me. I have overcome in many areas of my life just by speaking and believing the Word. As we proclaim God's Word, we are making a statement that we believe what God says according to scripture and It is extremely powerful. Thanks be to God for He gives us victory through our Lord Jesus Christ! I have been delivered from fear, drugs, and shame because God's word has delivering power. As I read, believed and received the Word, it gave me abilities to overcome obstacles and it strengthened areas of weakness. Just as Jesus countered satan's attack in the wilderness with the Word so should we.

> *Then Jesus said to him, "Away with you, satan! For it is written, 'You shall worship the Lord your God, and Him only you shall serve.'" (Matt 4:10)*

Over the years, my mind has been renewed by the Word washing over it, cleaning it of thoughts of doubt and unbelief. It changes old mindsets and gives a renewed way of thinking. I truly love God's Word! As we establish the Word in our lives we can stand on the Word and make declarations over our lives and our family. His Gospel does not just come in word only but in power also! (1 Thes 1:5) As we walk in the fullness of what God has given us, we are able to overcome anything we might encounter in our lives.

Jesus teaches us that we must live by every word from God! Our connection with God becomes this rich fulfilling relationship as we experience Him in all His ways. This is the abundant life! Both the written Word (logos) and the rhema Word has power beyond belief! We must hear His voice using His words as a powerful sword during our battles.

But He answered and said, "It is written, 'Man shall not live by bread alone, but by every word that proceeds from the mouth of God.' (Matt 4:4)

God speaks in so many ways and we should never limit Him by narrow beliefs. I have great hope that readers of this book will recognize that there is so much more that we as believers are able to walk in and move in with freedom. As we diligently seek Him, we will find Him! I want the body of believers to realize that God has so much more that He wants to do through us than we are experiencing. It is in us to walk in signs, wonders and miracles! We are a people that should be hearing the Father's voice. It is in us to move mountains! The same Spirit that raised Jesus from the dead resides in us, therefore we must hone in on what He is doing and join Him. I do not say this in a prideful way! Since He showed me that He wanted to do greater things I feel obligated to pass that message on. The Lord had me write this book to share some possibilities that maybe you might not have considered. I know I certainly never considered that communion with God could be so intimate or personal. Amazingly, He uses each of us uniquely. He may never do what He has done with me, but, for certain, He will do above what you can imagine or think. Furthermore, whatever The Lord does, it is for His grand plan!

The Lord helped me in many ways throughout all my years of teaching. He would give me ideas in the morning, as I laid in bed before getting up, for work. He gave me new and fun ideas for teaching too. Creativity came through ideas just as I would awaken. As crazy as it may seem, I sometimes saw myself wearing certain items of clothing. I'd get up and dress like I saw myself. Once, the Lord gave me an idea how to impart the Word to my students. Ways to show kindness, wisdom to deal with others, and how to show respect, are all topics in the Bible. I took a scripture that depicted a skill I felt my students needed to work on and displayed it on a poster in slightly simpler terms. That would be the skill we would work on for the week. We read the scripture frequently throughout the week and came up with ways to demonstrate the skill. At the end of the day the students were given time to give praise to any classmates exhibiting those skills. God's idea worked wonders in the classroom. His Word is powerful and when it is promoted it creates a loving, caring, and respectful environment. I saw a difference in behavior in the classroom and my students were also learning scripture. For those that think you cannot teach God's Word in public school. Think again!

Often, we have such high expectations on others that they are never able to fill them. Many of those expectations can only be filled by the Lord. When we continue to expect family, friends or spouses to fill those voids our disappointments mount and feelings of being let down accumulate. Eventually, people experience feelings of frustration or defeat. The first couple of years in my marriage I started feeling all these ways. Bitterness and resentment began to accrue placing a toll on my marriage. When one day as I was sitting in Sunday school with my husband, I heard the Lord speak these words to me. He said to just love him. It did not matter how I felt about our relationship, I was told to just love him. I knew that the Lord was telling me that my only job was to show my husband love.

I also began to pray that God would fill my husband and I with love for each other and I could literally feel that prayer kick in each time I prayed it. Whenever I felt like I needed more I drew more from the Lord. Instead of feeling anger over unmet expectations I found myself letting God fill in all the voids. I found out that God never disappointed me, and He never left me unfulfilled. Those simple words that the Holy Spirit whispered to me in Sunday school changed the way I responded and changed my life.

The Lord has more than we can envision to take care of every need that we have. He really can do that better than any one person. As we love others unconditionally, we are promised to reap the benefit. Draw upon the Lord whenever there is lack and He will bless abundantly. The Lord is our *source* and as He completes us, He causes us to overcome.

Worship is another place that helps me to overcome feelings of being overwhelmed with the pressures of this world. As we lift our heart toward Him and get our minds off the problem, we can recede into a beautiful place where He meets us through worship. Our attitude and emotions get in check as we lay it all down to a loving and caring God. He bestows peace where peace is hard to find. He is the Prince of Peace and as we give Him more of our selves through worship, we will find peace! There is something supernatural about being in His presence. It is where deep hurts disappear, and love reappears. It is where the storm gets calmed. As we worship the Lord in our own home or corporately, we can spend moments abandoning ourselves for a lifetime of adopting His nature. The more we focus solely on the Lord through worship with our love and adorations all our problems, fears, worries and needs fade. As we yield during worship the Holy Spirit becomes stirred within us. I find that I experience many facets of God such as joy, love and even revelation during worship. The garment of praise is wonderful to help release a spirit of heaviness.

> *To console those who mourn in Zion, to give them beauty for ashes, the oil of joy for mourning, The garment of praise for the spirit of heaviness; That they may be called trees of righteousness, The planting of the Lord, that He may be glorified." (Is. 61:3)*

For me, prayer helps me to overcome. Talking to the Father is vital in this rich relationship. As I pray, I am fixed on others which takes the focus off myself and helps me from being self-centered. I am very adamant on allowing the Holy Spirit to reveal things to me through prayer rather than praying solely from my own thoughts or lists. I pray using the Holy Spirit's language allowing Him to begin flowing through me. As I pray, I give the Holy Spirit opportunity to reveal whatever is needed for intercession.

Over the years I have either been in a prayer group or led one. There has never been a time when I left prayer time feeling empty, sad or burdened. In fact, I feel pumped up, uplifted, and built up. It is exhilarating and energizing! Others I pray with usually say the same thing. It does not make sense! In God's kingdom, the more you do to fulfill your call the more invigorating it becomes. It is incredible! I find that the people I pray with I tend to have the closest relationships. I feel such a bond with those I pray with because we enter a secret place together. I encourage you to find a prayer partner. You will find a lifelong friend and someone that in whom you can trust. Prayer creates an atmosphere to overcome the enemy and to feel that ever increasing faith.

> *And take the helmet of salvation, and the sword of the Spirit, which is the word of God; praying always with all prayer and supplication in the Spirit, being watchful to this end with all perseverance and supplication for all the saints (Eph 6:16-18)*

CHAPTER 22

Evidence That God Calls Us into Ministry

"The Spirit of the Lord is upon Me, Because He has anointed Me To preach the gospel to the poor; He has sent Me to heal the brokenhearted, to proclaim liberty to the captives and recovery of sight to the blind, to set at liberty those who are oppressed; (Luke 4:18)

God has been calling people to accomplish His purposes and plans since the beginning. God called Abraham, Noah and Moses to set in motion great feats. The Bible is full of people being called whether by God, Jesus or the Holy Spirit. There are many examples of each. Jesus called the disciples as He taught them and trained them on earth before He ascended to the Father. Even today, people are being called for kingdom purposes. Some calls are quite dramatic such as Saul's conversion (becoming Paul). Jesus extraordinarily appeared to Paul on the road to Emmaus and even blinded him. Some people are moved gradually into the call of God. I have had both experiences as I have received various calls on my life. I find that the above scripture is certain, however, the Lord places variances within that call.

Many people are called to minister to their family and may not minister to a great degree outside the home. The call of God for ministry might be within the workplace. Some might be drawn to minister to and provide for the homeless where another might be drawn to teach and train teenagers. The call of God is extremely diverse, and we must value each other for the variety of differences. We need each other to form a complete body of ministries. If you are unsure of the call of God on your life seek Him diligently and He will faithfully show you your place. Not all fall within the five-fold ministries of pastors, teachers, evangelists, prophets and apostles. God's call is as varied as the needs of people.

> *And the Lord called Samuel again the third time. Then he arose and went to Eli, and said, "Here I am, for you did call me." Then Eli perceived that the Lord had called the boy. (1Sam. 3:8)*

While seeking the Lord, He gave me an illustration showing me how I would recognize His call. While praying I saw complete darkness in a vision. I heard distant screams and cries for help from a pit in the darkness. I saw myself go to where I heard the screams and reach my hand down and start pulling people out of the pit. The Lord told me that I would know where to go because I would hear the cries of the people. I am often reminded of this vision and the words of the Lord. It's hard to dispel the screams of those people needing help. Today, I hear the cries of children caught in pedophilia and trafficking. I pray, I spread awareness, and donate money to groups aggressively trying to rescue these little ones. I do all I know to do.

God uses you and I to rescue those caught in the pit!

The call to minister in prison was a gradual one for me. When I first became a Christian, I constantly prayed that God would tell me what my ministry was, so I could do what I was supposed to do. I worked in the nursery several years at my church but knew there had to be more for me to do. I sought the Lord, earnestly, concerning my call for ministry. I remember early on having this strong desire to go to prisons. I kept thinking how I really wanted to do ministry in prison which seemed strange to me to have that desire. I would even tell people that I had an interest in prison ministry and when I would say the words, they seemed foreign to me. Why did I want to go to prison? I didn't know anyone in prison. I did not have any connections to people that were in prison nor did I know people that broke the law. I was an unassuming person that taught first grade and felt very inadequate to have the ability to minister to people in prison, yet I had this strong desire. The desire just didn't fit the picture, although I had this drawing to do prison ministry. I didn't even like being called to the office at work. God is intriguing like that! Since He created each of us, He knows more of what we are suited for than we know ourselves. He just drops something in your spirit and then watches to see what you do with it.

Approximately four years later I was standing in my classroom placing some papers in the filing cabinet when in walks Judy, a coworker. We began a conversation and she seemed very excited about Jesus. We continued to discuss some experiences she was having, and she mentioned prison. She had the opportunity to go into solitary confinement to pray for women through her church, with Emmaus Walk. She must have noticed my peak in interest when she mentioned prison. Therefore, she asked me if I would want to go into a women's prison with her to pray. I enthusiastically responded with a yes! I told her that I had always wanted to go to prison and I didn't really know why I had that desire.

So, a few weeks later we started ministry to women in prison. I was scared every time I went into prison for the first year. I had never been in a prison and it was very intimidating. My greatest fear was how the women would respond to us. I thought women would yell at us and maybe even curse us. That could not be further from the truth. The women were opened-armed and very kind to us.

In fact, the women are very appreciative that we come. My friend and I get significantly blessed every time we go. God touches our hearts as much as the women we minister to. Our sole ministry is to pray with women. Many people go into prison to minister, but I don't hear that they are allowed to go into solitary. This call to ministry is perfect for me because of my love for prayer and because I have a heart for women. God placed that desire to minister in prison in me long ago for a purpose. He then opened the door to accomplish His purpose. He amazes me how He orchestrates us as we are willing to be moved. God opened the doors for us to minister in solitary confinement and I am grateful that He continues to keep the door open. It has been 17 years that Judy and I have been going and we love it! My daughter has just begun going in to pray with us. I am excited to see the next generation stepping into that call of God!

As I have explained previously, the call to pray came immediately after receiving the infilling of the Holy Spirit and it began to build and increase over the years. We are all called to pray, but I always seemed to have had an additional urgency to pray for others. I had this earnestness to pray in the language of the Holy Spirit and also in the understanding (English). This call to prayer has increased over the years. At first, I only prayed privately in my own home then it branched out into praying on teams. Both are very powerful! I have enjoyed prayer walking in my community seeking God for wisdom and have met with other intercessors for prayer assignments. The Lord would impress one of the intercessors to go somewhere and several of us would join in to pray. I spent three years on a team traveling in the state of Indiana with Sally Burton and the Strategic Prayer Network. That was very exciting to pray for my home state. We traveled with a spontaneous, prophetic worship group led by a man named Gregg Jackson. The prayer and worship team came together alongside one another and were led by the Holy Spirit to pray and worship for our state. It was tremendously powerful!

The Lord has called me into several directions, and it has been an extremely exciting life. Did I tell you, already that it's been an exciting life? Sometimes, one call will lead you into another branch of that initial call. When He began to teach me to hear His voice it led me into opportunities to teach. Doors opened to teach and share with groups of women. Public speaking has always been a challenge, but I could not say no when there was so much to share about this Great God, Jehovah! Thankfully, once I start talking about Jesus and all He has done the nervousness fades. I can teach whatever I need to, but the fire ignites with sharing what the Lord burns within my heart. I have enjoyed teaching at many retreats and ministering by the Holy Spirit in women's meetings. God will use us in areas of our greatest weaknesses. Moses too felt inadequate to speak before others, but God wants to show us that in our weaknesses He is strong.

The Lord, by His Spirit, brings His people to that place where He is in us and we are in Him. We are one! It is a place of perfect unity and a place of the highest feeling of fulfillment. I recognize that God is working through us to do mighty things on this earth. As we humble ourselves and allow Him to show us what He has prepared for each of us we will experience complete contentment. I encourage you to seek God for your purpose if you haven't found that place yet. I realize that if nothing is happening in our life, spiritually, it's because the Lord is waiting on us.

I am the vine, you are the branches. He who abides in Me, and I in him, bears much fruit; for without Me you can do nothing. (John 15:5)

He must become greater; I must become less." (John 3:30)

Sometimes the call of God stems out of an experience that we have had. I had such a wonderful experience from getting baptized in the Holy Spirit that I instantly began to tell people about it. I found out quickly that just as me they had never heard of being baptized in the Holy Spirit. It became a challenge as I tried to explain to them how wonderful it was and how empowered I had become because of this encounter so I began studying all about it in the Bible.

My aunt was sure my mother and I had gotten into a cult, but it wasn't long before she got saved and baptized in the Holy Spirit also. As I began to tell people about what Jesus had said about receiving the Holy Spirit, I in turn started praying for people to receive the infilling of the Holy Spirit. Each time they would receive and would begin speaking in that beautiful heavenly language. I encouraged people to receive it because of the great value in it. If Jesus stated that we needed to be filled with His Spirit, then I realized how important it was. This was my rationalization and understanding, so I began placing a high importance on it too. I rarely pray with anyone for salvation without telling them about receiving the empowerment of the Holy Spirit simultaneously.

I also spent many times ministering alongside my mother. She too placed a high importance on being filled with the Holy Spirit. I was with her on many occasions as she prayed for people to be filled with God's Holy Spirit. People were moved tremendously as they were baptized with the Spirit. The look on their faces was priceless. I often cried tears of joy as each person received God's beautiful gift of the Holy Spirit. I believe God calls us all to pray for people to be filled with the Holy Spirit, but most are timid about telling others about the third part of the Godhead. I assume it is because they do not have enough understanding.

Behold, I send the Promise of My Father upon you; but tarry in the city of Jerusalem until you are endued with power from on high." (Luke 24:49)

Because of these fabulous experiences I have a strong call to pray with others to receive the infilling of the Holy Spirit. I know how vital the Holy Spirit is to the believer. Jesus said the Holy Spirit would teach, comfort, reveal truth and would endue us with power. I also had a dream that confirmed the call of God on my life. In the dream, I proclaimed that the baptism of the Holy Spirit was my message. I recognize this as to be truth.

Examine your heart to see what tugs on it and I believe you will find the beginning of what you are called to. God places desires in our heart and places breadcrumbs for us to follow. He is a loving God that passes His love to us and through us. He knows us intricately because He created us, therefore He knows exactly what each of us is suited for even when we are clueless. When I became a Christian, I was vastly clueless of my capabilities. My mind was limited to what I could do and not what I could do with Him. Whatever it takes, seek Him for your call. I still seek Him for our next move toward whatever is on His heart.

Through Him we have received grace and apostleship for obedience to the faith among all nations for His name, among whom you also are the called of Jesus Christ; To all who are in Rome, beloved of God, called to be saints: Grace to you and peace from God our Father and the Lord Jesus Christ. (Ro.1:5-7)

CHAPTER 23

Evidence That God Warns

Now when they had departed, behold, an angel of the Lord appeared to Joseph in a dream, saying, "Arise, take the young Child and His mother, flee to Egypt, and stay there until I bring you word; for Herod will seek the young Child to destroy Him." (Matt 2:13)

God has warned people throughout the Bible. He warned Mary and Joseph to escape to Egypt after Jesus was born to take Jesus to safety. Jonah was sent to Nineveh to issue a warning to the people that if they did not repent, they would be destroyed. Jonah severely fought against being obedient and ended up in the belly of the whale. He, eventually, went to the city and issued God's warning. The people repented, and God spared the city.

I have received a hand full of warnings. Some were for other people and some were for me personally. I always think these warnings are very important and take them very seriously. Sometimes people take heed to these warnings and sometimes they don't. If God sends out a warning it could be as serious as a life and death matter or it could be to spare us from added pain and suffering.

Many years ago, my younger brother answered an ad in the newspaper to go to Alabama for a job. There were not many details in the article but listed the pay and that they would provide a place for him to live. Once he responded to the advertisement, he found out that they would include paying for the travel expenses getting there. Consequently, he asked my parents to take him to Alabama. I found this very alarming even though my brother was in his twenties. I felt adamant that my brother was not supposed to go. I kept urging him not to go through several phone conversations. At that time, in my walk with the Lord, I did not completely recognize it being God's warning, but I continued to feel disturbed over this whole situation. My parents were going to drive him down with his cat along with his things and drop him off.

The night before he left I, once again, urged him not to go. I plead with him not to go. I became adamant with him and made a bold statement. I told him that if he went that I did not think he would come back and that he would die. Well, to my dismay he still would not listen to me and left early the next morning with my parents.

After many hours of driving they finally arrived at a dumpy, unkept trailer in Alabama. My brother placed his cat inside and spoke to the man on the property that had placed the ad for Mike to come down and work. The man gave Mike the gas money and he in turn gave it to my parents. My mother felt very unsettled about leaving him and questioned him several times by asking him if he was sure he wanted to do this. Mike assured her that he wanted to stay even though he was feeling a bit skittish himself. My father had been a truck driver for many years and was familiar with the area and mentioned that they could all go to lunch at this great place to eat down the road. When they arrived, my father went to talk to the owner of the place that he knew. When he explained the whole situation to the owner at the truck stop, he also told him the man's name that had put out the ad. My dad's friend had a strong reaction and told him to take his son back home. He told him that the guy was up on several charges and that he was the biggest kingpin of corruption in that area!

My parents hurriedly drove back to the trailer, picked up the cat and took off toward home. That was a huge ordeal and truly scared my brother and all of us. I often think about that and how God protected my brother from something that day. Knowing about the big business of human trafficking I honestly think that is what was going down. We all realized that God warned us, and I thank God He did not stop warning until someone listened.

God warns in various other ways such as through dreams, visions and even by sending angels. The warning about my brother was discernment. My brother thought I was just being an overprotective big sister. I knew

I was having a strong feeling about the Alabama situation, but I was not sure it was the Lord. It is vital that we learn the Father's voice because He always knows what is ahead and wants to spare us from tragedy.

When Abraham and Sarah were traveling, they were stopped by a group of men in Gerar. Abraham stated that Sarah was his sister as he recognized the interest they had in her. The men saw how beautiful Sarah was and King Abimelech sent for her to be brought to him. God intervened on behalf of Sarah and Abraham. That night King Abimelech received a warning to return the woman or he and his household would die. He promptly did so, and all was well (Gen 20:3).

I had approximately three to four dreams about being distracted while driving in my van. Each time I would be reaching down to pick something up off the floorboard of my vehicle I would go over a cliff and every time I would awaken as I was plummeting over a cliff. One of the times in a dream, I opened my van door and was reaching down onto the road to pick up a snake when I then headed over into a ravine. I knew it was a stern warning from the Lord. I still get distracted at times and I always snap back to being mindful of the warnings, especially being deceived by the snake. My home is atop of a knob and I travel up and down the knobs daily. This was a significant warning that I took seriously. Often, God's warnings are not adhered to and grave circumstances occur.

I had a very severe warning for my two youngest children while they were still in high school. It was a very detailed dream. I heard my daughter's name being called out in the dream making me aware who this dream was about. Me, my son and daughter were making our way along a rocky edge and I was showing them the way to get to the other side without falling. When, suddenly, my son stands up and dives over the cliff to his death. As soon as this occurs my daughter follows in suit and dives over the cliff as if to follow her brother. The one followed the other one, completely without thinking. In the dream I could not understand why they did this. I questioned in the dream whether they misunderstood me on the way to go. I had been trying to get them to grab ahold of the branches of this tree as the rocks were giving away beneath them. I also saw more details concerning each one of them pertaining to their future.

When I woke up, I typed up every detail and called them together to share my warning. I read them the dream and I gave them a copy of it.

They were teenagers and they did not pay much attention to the warning. Once they got out of high school, they began to make some bad choices. The following years became a nightmare for them both as they fell into drug addiction. My son and daughter did not listen and they both came close to dying through their addictions and activity. Just like in the dream neither of them listened to my direction toward Christianity and following the Lord. It took many years of pain and suffering before they turned back around serving the Lord. Like I said, sometimes warnings are listened to and sometimes they are not. Their disobedience caused many years of grief for our entire family. My daughter is now a strong Christian woman and helps others out of addiction, therefore, I see where God brings good out of the worst situations. Even Pharaoh did not listen to Moses' warning and horrible things happened to him, his family and the people. Many curses fell upon them all because of disobeying a warning from God.

Another time I received a warning by vision to a church. That was the only time I had a warning for a church. I was driving late at night and had been praying many hours in the car when I had a vision of my church. I saw the church building shoot up into the sky with expediency and growth. It shot up into the sky so quickly that I gasped because I recognized that it was toppling because of the weak foundation. The type of foundation was not set in place to uphold the growth. The Lord then showed me where chicken wire should be laid for the foundation. The chicken wire symbolized prayer cells. Chicken wire has shapes that are circular throughout and I knew that the church needed to create prayer cells to bring stability. Then, I saw concrete poured in the cells for that foundation. There were many people interested in praying at that time where it would not have taken much to set up prayer teams. The word was rejected, and it was stated that the church was working on Sunday school. References to a former church were made where they had such prayer cells. I got the impression that the pastor had been hurt somehow concerning the prayer. It was not but three years and the whole thing toppled. It was a shame because at that time there were three services going and it all collapsed, and the pastor was asked to leave. Was it solely because of disobedience to that warning? I doubt it! God usually sends several warnings. All I know is that I saw it collapse and it was so alarming that I went to meet with a pastor. That took some bravery on my part because I had never done anything like that before.

Each of us plays only a small part to what God is doing. Being obedient to that one part is all we are accountable. Warnings from God are serious!

I do not usually have repetitive dreams other than the driving off the cliff dreams, but I have had several dreams that I sold my house. Each time I grieve over selling my house and each time I spend the whole dream hoping I can buy it back. Crazy dream! I do not have a very big house and it was built in the seventies, so it isn't one of great beauty or of great value. But I truly feel that I am never to sell my house. I believe these dreams of my house are a warning from the Lord.

One time I was on a trip with a friend and it was the final morning of our trip. Early one morning before light I awoke with an intense fear. I travel frequently and have never felt fear like that in a hotel room. I prayed and commanded the fear to go but it was so intense, and I could not get relief of it. Moments later, I heard a man and woman, a couple of rooms down, begin to fight. They were yelling back and forth. I could hear it getting physical according to the noises. It was very heated and for some reason I kept feeling we needed to get out of there, NOW! I woke my friend up and I told her about my experience and then about the big fight between the couple. I was still shaking but it went quiet between the couple. We hurriedly gathered our things and I insisted that we go the other direction away from the couple that had been fighting. We went down the back stairs and got out of there quickly. All this seemed odd to me, but I knew the Lord was warning me of something. To this day, I am not quite sure of the details of that situation, but it was such a strong warning with confirming signs that I knew what I needed to do.

Two or three months after becoming a Christian and being filled with the Holy Spirit I was praying persistently. Being single at the time gave me a lot of free time. I spent one hour, then two hours praying in tongues and in English. There is such a power in that, and I wish the body of Christ would embrace the concept of that amazing power. After praying for that length of time I found myself laying on the living room floor of my apartment. There was such a holiness surrounding me and I felt the presence of God particularly intimate. I heard Him speaking to me ever so gently. I had this overwhelming realization that I had God's undivided attention, so I asked Him a question. The question was very personal concerning an incident that had happened with a boyfriend. Since I had received salvation and been filled with the Holy Spirit, I had kept myself pure from sexual activity except for this one time.

I lay there in the quietness of God's glorious presence for quite some time. It was so beautiful and sweet being surrounded by Him. Seeing that I had God's attention, I asked Him if this sexual activity would keep me from going to heaven. I heard a still, quiet voice answer yes. After this response from the Lord I then placed a request on the response. I said, "Lord, I really know this is you, but will you *pierce* my right side, so I will know for sure that this would keep me from going to heaven." I immediately received a sharp piercing to my right rib area. I was completely surprised at the response of the Lord and that He would acknowledge my request. To completely assure myself I repeated, "Lord, I really know this is You, but could you assure me for the second time and pierce my side telling me this would keep me from going to heaven?" Immediately, for the second time the Lord pierced my right rib area with a sharp pain. I was equally as stunned the second time. I was shocked, for one, that the Lord was speaking to me and that I heard Him so clearly. Most of all I was astounded that He would respond with a physical warning. It was an emphatic answer from the Lord that I was not to be engaged in fornication.

God is such a loving Father and wants the best for each of us. For Him to warn me in that manner was life changing. I certainly don't think I thought of that myself about being pierced in the side. I believe the Holy Spirit led me to pray that because He wanted me to know the will of the Father. When I encounter unmarried couples living together, I tell them this story as I am led by the Holy Spirit. I certainly listened to this warning for my life.

One night I was sound asleep and was awakened by some loud whisperings beside my bed. I discerned three demonic entities on my side of the bed whispering. My husband was not awakened by this activity, but I jumped out of bed and recognized that it was a spirit of death. I began praying and casting death out of my house. I must add that I never felt fear but felt extremely empowered! I walked throughout my house and into the basement to command the spirit of death to leave. After I prayed for some time and prayed for protection from the Lord I, peacefully, went back to bed. Obviously, there was a plot against my life or my husband's life. I know some type of demonic activity was thwarted because of this discernment.

I had never had the gifting of discerning of spirits operate to that degree before, but because the Holy Spirit revealed it to me, I knew what I was encountering. The gifts are very important and are evidence of the Holy Spirit's operation. I find that some of the Holy Spirit's gifts run strong through me, but I believe all believers can operate in every one of them. They will manifest when they are needed. We must value the Holy Spirit giftings. The gifts are just a few characteristics of the Holy Spirit that empowers the believer. As we operate in these gifts and mature in moving in them the world gets a clearer view of Jesus' nature and His demeanor.

But the manifestation of the Spirit is given to each one for the profit of all: for to one is given the word of wisdom through the Spirit, to another the word of knowledge through the same Spirit, to another faith by the same Spirit, to another gifts of healings by the same Spirit, to another the working of miracles, to another prophecy, to another discerning of spirits, to another different kinds of tongues, to another the interpretation of tongues. But one and the same Spirit works all these things, <u>distributing to each one individually as He wills</u>. (1 Cor 12:9-11)

CHAPTER 24

Evidence That God Is A Generational God

I have no greater joy than to hear that my children walk in truth.
(3 John1:4)

I sat in the nursing home looking into the disappointed face of my best friend, my mother. She laid dying of cancer and she did not have long to live according to the doctors. I knew she had expected to live many more years. She had plans. She anticipated more to come! She had considerable expectations to fulfill all that her Lord had placed within her heart and, somehow, all was ending abruptly.

I could feel her pain…as if there was more to complete, more to accomplish. I could see it within her countenance. Assuredly, the pain and suffering of cancer was enough, but there it was, an obvious agony that maybe only I could recognize because of our closeness, our complete understanding of one another. I knew she was feeling extremely let down, disappointed. Although, we never spoke of it even though we shared everything and loved talking about every minute detail about our Lord.

I have thought of that moment over and over and have had difficulty forgetting it. It seemed to be something important. For me to dwell on it so frequently it must be important, something God wanted me to know. God was teaching me something in that moment as well as He was for her. What was it? As I looked at my own life, I too knew some day it was going to all end. Would I feel that same disappointment of not being able to complete all God had placed in my heart to complete?

Even though It took me several years to understand what He was trying to say, I realize its importance for me and maybe it will be important for you too. We are never finished! In fact, our vision, our call becomes something we pass on. My mom passed on her faith to me. She passed on her hope to see greater signs and wonders and miracles. She passed on the love for people and her desire to help them grow spiritually. We can relax, trust God, and realize we only complete our part. I see it in my children. I see how they take pieces of what God imparted to me and then He builds in them their specific call. It's how God works. He works and does for the greater picture, for the fulfillment of His divine purpose.

He is a Generational God!

And I will establish My covenant between Me and you and your descendants after you in their generations, for an everlasting covenant, to be God to you and your descendants after you. (Gen. 17:7)

What a relief that gives me because I had the feeling, I was running out of time to fulfill God's call on my life. I know my mom had that same feeling because we are so much alike. We are to press toward that mark of the prize of the high calling and never stop until He says we are finished with our part. He continues to give us a hope and a future and draws us as if it were the first day, we met Him. He gives us new nuggets, fresh visions and hopeful dreams. As we look at Jesus' life and purpose here on earth, we see He was NOT finished until IT WAS FINISHED. From that point He passed it all to us! Even on the cross He was mandating things. John was to look after His mother. He was asking the Father to forgive those around Him for they did not know what they were doing. He encouraged one of the thieves on the cross next to Him by saying, "Surely you will be in paradise this day!"

It's amazing how far He takes us and how individually and uniquely He teaches each one of us. I wish I could have alleviated my mom's pain by encouraging her with this revelation. I wish I would have told her that she was such a powerful example for her children and her grandchildren and that she impacted the generations to come. And that we would carry all those things forward because of her faithfulness. I wish I could have told her those things. Jesus has taken over now, and I don't have to worry about incomplete words.

I'm sure she heard the words as she stood before Him,

"Well done good and faithful servant!"

So much of my story I owe to her. It was because of her Christian example that I did not know what she had, but I wanted it. She helped me to understand the importance of confessing Jesus before others. She also explained the delivering power of our heavenly Father, so that I would ask for it. She told me about the Holy Spirit, so that I would know to seek and receive His empowerment. She held my hand as a friend and a confidant and taught me what a relationship with God looked like. Foundationally, she helped me get started on this thirty-four-year journey. We all have people that made a difference in our lives and I give honor to my mom!

God used my mom to open doors and then He came in and showed me all that was available in all the rooms to the house of God. What a life this has been thus far. I am looking forward to the years ahead, awaiting the next new surprise, the next word of direction or the next dream or vision. I earnestly look forward to seeing the lives the Lord transforms and the hearts He captivates. I anticipate seeing the directions He takes my children and how He reveals Himself, uniquely, to and through them.

It's A Wonderful Life!

OTHER BOOKS BY
SHIRLEY HALL

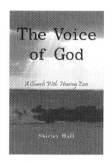

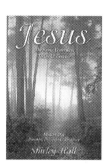

Printed in the United States
By Bookmasters